FACTS AT YOUR FINGERTIPS

INTRODUCING CHEMISTRY
ORGANIC CHEMISTRY AND BIOCHEMISTRY

BROWN
BEAR
BOOKS

CONTENTS

Published by Brown Bear Books Limited

4877 N. Circulo Bujia
Tucson, AZ 85718
USA

and

First Floor
9-17 St. Albans Place
London N1 ONX
UK
www.brownreference.com

© 2010 The Brown Reference Group Ltd

Library of Congress Cataloging-in-Publication Data

Organic chemistry and biochemistry / edited by Graham Bateman.
   p. cm. — (Facts at your fingertips)
  Includes index.
  ISBN 978-1-936333-14-1 (library binding)
 1. Chemistry, Organic. 2. Biochemistry. I. Bateman, Graham. II.
Title. III. Series.

  QD253.2.O68 2010
  547—dc22

    47648576 1/12 2010016456

ISBN-13 978-1-936333-14-1

Editorial Director: Lindsey Lowe
Project Director: Graham Bateman
Design Manager: David Poole
Designers: Steve McCurdy, Martin Anderson
Picture Researchers: Steve McCurdy, Graham Bateman
Text Editor: Briony Ryles
Indexer: David Bennett
Children's Publisher: Anne O'Daly
Production Director: Alastair Gourlay

Printed in the United States of America

Picture Credits
Abbreviations: SS=Shutterstock; c=center; t=top; l=left; r=right.

Cover Images
Front: SS: Fotocrisis
Back: SS: Montenegro

1 SS: Dr. Margorius; 3 SS: Socrates; 4-5 SS: Siloto; 6-7 Wikimedia
Commons: United States Navy; 9 SS: Norman Pogson; 11 SS:
Punksid; 12-13 Wikimedia Commons: United States Navy; 14 SS:
Photofish; 17 SS: Ronald Caswell; 18 SS: Design 56; 20 SS:
Martin D. Vonka; 22 SS: Andrey Pavlov; 23 SS: Elnur; 24-25 SS:
Graeme Dawes; 25 Wikimedia Commons: Hamon jp; 27 SS:
Micha Pucha; 28l SS: Aiti; 28r SS: Micha Rosenwirth; 31
Photos.com; 33 SS: Eric Wong; 34 SS: Dr. Margorius; 35 SS:
Stephen Bures; 36 SS: DDCoral; 37 Wikimedia Commons: Kiselov
Yuri; 38 SS: Tischenko Irina; 39 SS: Christopher Elwell; 41 SS:
Dundanim; 43 SS: Maria Dryfhout; 47 SS: Pavzyuk Svitlana; 49
SS: Ifong; 50 Wikimedia Commons: Nephron; 52 SS: Socrates; 53
Wikimedia Commons: Kaim-Martin Knaak; 54 Wikimedia
Commons: Ninjatacoshell; 55 SS: Bogdan Wankowicz; 56 SS:
Shah Rohani; 57 Wikimedia Commons: Mnolf; 58 Wikimedia
Commons: Guillaume Paumier; 59 SS: Susan Flashman; 60
Wikimedia Commons: United States Department of Agriculture.

Artwork © The Brown Reference Group Ltd

*The Brown Reference Group Ltd has made every effort to trace
copyright holders of the pictures used in this book. Anyone having
claims to ownership not identified above is invited to contact The
Brown Reference Group Ltd.*

Facts at your Fingertips—Introducing Chemistry describes the essentials of chemistry from the fundamentals of atomic structure, through the periodic table, to descriptions of different types of reactions and the properties of elements, including industrial applications for chemical processes.

The element carbon is unique—its compounds are the foundation of all life on Earth, as well as occurring in a myriad of substances involved in our daily lives, from plastics to gasoline to drugs and food items. Most chemicals that contain carbon are called organic compounds. The discipline that involves the study of these is called organic chemistry, and the study of molecules and chemical reactions in living organisms is called biochemistry—both are the subject of this volume.

Numerous explanatory diagrams and informative photographs, detailed features on related aspects of the topics covered and the main scientists involved in the advancement of chemistry, and definitions of key "Science Words," all enhance the coverage. "Try This" features outline experiments that can be undertaken as a first step to practical investigations.

Chemists divide chemicals into two groups: organic and inorganic. Organic chemicals contain large amounts of carbon. They occur in everything from plastics to gasoline to drugs and even make up life-forms, including you!

When you are learning about chemistry, you are shown many examples of how atoms and molecules (atoms joined together) react with each other, and how their structures affect the way they behave. Most of these examples are very simple, so you can understand them easily. You learn about water, salt, and metals—substances that you come across everyday. However, most of the substances around you now are not so simple to make or easy to understand.

Complex chemicals

Living bodies—the most complex things in nature—and many of the most useful materials made by people, such as plastics, fuels, and drugs, are made from very complex compounds. Chemists describe the compounds

A pair of butterflies in the wild. Their bodies are made up of organic chemicals, such as sugars, proteins, and fats. All life on Earth is based on organic compounds.

SCIENCE WORDS

- **Atom:** The smallest piece of an element that still retains the properties of that element.
- **Biochemistry:** The study of chemical reactions inside bodies.
- **Compound:** A substance formed when atoms of two or more different elements bond together.
- **Inorganic:** Describes a substance that is not organic.
- **Molecule:** Two or more atoms connected by chemical bonds.
- **Organic:** Describes a compound that is made of carbon and generally also contains hydrogen.

as being organic. That is because those compounds that occur in nature have all originally been produced by living things.

A compound is a substance that is made when the atoms of two or more elements bond together. Organic compounds contain many atoms, even thousands, bonded together in a very precise pattern. All organic compounds are based on the element carbon (C). The compounds also contain atoms of other elements,

carbon and hydrogen atoms in an organic compound by measuring the amount of each of these gases produced when it burns.

In 1828, Friedrich Wöhler (1800-1882) discovered that organic compounds could be made from inorganic ones. Chemists began to look at organic compounds in a new way. They looked at simple compounds with just a few atoms in them. These included nut oils, formic acid made by stinging ants, and alcohol made by rotting fruit.

The chemists saw that some compounds react in the same ways even though they are very different in other ways. The scientists realized that these compounds all have the same group of atoms somewhere in their molecule. It is these so-called functional groups that give the compounds their properties. Today's organic chemists study how these functional groups work and even make up new ones.

DIVIDING CHEMISTRY

Chemists first studied organic compounds in the early 19th century, when people began investigating the substances inside the bodies of life-forms. Many believed that these compounds were so complex that they could only be made inside a living body, or organism. Because of this, Swedish chemist Jöns Jacob Berzelius (1779–1848) called the compounds organic. All other compounds were therefore inorganic. However, in 1828, the German chemist Friedrich Wöhler (1800–1882) showed that organic compounds could be made in a laboratory as well. He reacted two inorganic compounds together and, completely by accident, produced urea, a substance that occurs in urine. This discovery showed that organic compounds were built the same way as other compounds, but that they were just more complicated.

---

most often hydrogen (H), but oxygen (O), nitrogen (N), and chlorine (Cl) are also commonly involved.

Connecting sections

The first chemists to investigate organic compounds could not figure out much about them. The methods used for studying inorganic compounds did not work very well with organic ones. Chemists knew that organic compounds contained carbon and hydrogen because when the compounds burned, they produced water vapor (H_2O) and carbon dioxide (CO_2). Burning, or combustion, occurs when a compound reacts with oxygen. Chemists can calculate the proportions of

CARBON BONDING

All organic compounds contain carbon atoms. Carbon is the only element with atoms that can form limitless chains as well as branched and ring structures. This ability is a result of the way carbon forms bonds.

Outer electron

Inner electron

Electron shell

Nucleus

Carbon has two electron shells. The inner shell has two electrons and the outer shell has four electrons. These four electrons allow carbon to form single, double, or triple covalent bonds.

Organic compounds exist in a mind-boggling array of shapes and sizes. Their molecules often form chains, rings, and networks of the two, but there are also coiled molecules, spheres, and even tiny tubes. All this variety is a result of the ability of carbon atoms to form strong bonds. To understand how carbon atoms form so many molecules, it is worth looking at pure carbon itself.

Pure forms of carbon

Carbon occurs in nature in four main forms: soot, fullerenes, diamond, and graphite. Both soot and fullerenes are made when carbon-containing compounds are burned. Fullerenes are very fragile structures and were only discovered 20 years ago. Soot, a fine black powder also known as amorphous carbon, does not have an ordered structure; its carbon atoms are arranged randomly.

Graphite and diamond are the two most stable and familiar forms of pure carbon. Despite being made of nothing but carbon atoms, the two substances are very different.

Carbon atom

How can the atoms of one element make two so very different materials? The answer is in the way the atoms

Oil is a hydrocarbon. When it burns in air, it creates carbon dioxide, carbon monoxide, water, and pure carbon (soot). The black smoke in this oil well fire is composed of soot particles, which will settle on the ground as ash.

are connected inside each substance. To understand how carbon forms bonds, we must look inside an atom of carbon. Carbon atoms have four electrons in their outer shell. These electrons are the ones that form bonds with other atoms. Atoms form bonds by sharing, taking, or giving away their outer electrons. They do this to make their outer electron shell full, which makes the atoms stable.

An atom's outer shell can hold eight electrons. To become stable, a carbon atom must share four electrons with other atoms. A bond formed when atoms share electrons is called a covalent bond. Carbon atoms are unusual, however, because their outer shell is half full (or half empty). That makes the atoms more stable than most. As a result carbon atoms can form two or even three strong bonds with just one other atom. Carbon's ability to form so-called double and triple bonds is behind the differences between graphite, diamond, and other forms of pure carbon.

CARBON AND COVALENT BONDS

A carbon atom can form up to four covalent bonds. These bonds involve two atoms sharing electrons. In a simple covalent bond, each atom provides one electron, forming a pair. The pair of electrons sits in the outer shell of both atoms. As a result the atoms are pulled side by side. The shared pair of electrons is being pulled on by the positive charge of the nucleus of both atoms. These pulling forces hold, or bond, the atoms together. This arrangement is called a single bond.

A carbon atom can form two or three bonds with one other atom. These are known as double and triple bonds. Most of the time, double and triple bonds form between two carbon atoms.

In a double bond, each atom shares two of its electrons. A triple bond involves three pairs. Compounds with double and triple bonds are more reactive than those with single bonds. The bonds often break so they can form more stable single bonds.

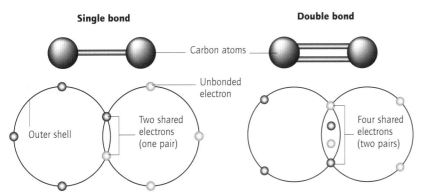

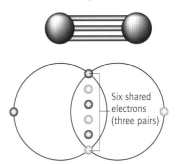

Single bond

Carbon atoms

Unbonded electron

Outer shell

Two shared electrons (one pair)

Double bond

Four shared electrons (two pairs)

Triple bond

Six shared electrons (three pairs)

In a single bond, each atom gives one electron, forming a pair shared between both of the atoms. The atoms' other electrons are free to form bonds with other atoms.

In a double bond, each atom gives two electrons, forming two pairs of shared electrons. The bond pulls the two atoms closer together than in a single bond.

In a triple bond, each atom gives three electrons, forming three pairs shared between them. The bond pulls the two atoms even closer together.

Different bonds

Inside a diamond, carbon atoms are connected by only single bonds. Each carbon atom is bonded to the four atoms surrounding it. With all the atoms bonded to one another, a piece of diamond is one huge molecule.

Diamond's extreme hardness is a result of its atoms being bonded into a rigid interconnecting structure. Graphite is so soft and different from diamond in many other ways because some of the atoms inside are joined by a weaker type of bond.

Inside graphite, each carbon is joined to just three atoms by single bonds. The atom is also connected to a fourth atom, but this time the bond is a weak bond that forms in the same way as a double bond. However, the bond in graphite is not quite the same because only one pair of electrons is shared.

This fourth bond is very weak, and as a result the carbon atoms inside graphite are not as strongly connected to each other. When a force pushes on graphite, it breaks the atoms' weak bonds easily, and the graphite breaks or changes shape. A lump of graphite feels slippery. That is because even the touch of your fingers is enough to rub away a layer of graphite. Graphite is used as a lubricant instead of oil or grease.

Carrying electricity

The structure of graphite also explains how it carries electricity, though diamond cannot. An electric current is a flow of electrons—sometimes other charged particles—through a substance. The moving particles transfer energy from one place to another, and electric currents are used to power many machines in our homes, schools, and places of work.

Substances that can carry electricity are conductors; they have electrons that are free to move around inside. Insulators—materials that do not carry electricity—do not have free electrons. Graphite is a conductor

SCIENCE WORDS

- **Allotrope:** One form of a pure element.
- **Conductor:** A substance that carries electricity and heat well.
- **Covalent bond:** A bond in which two or more atoms share electrons.
- **Crystal:** A solid made of repeating patterns of atoms.
- **Electron shell:** A layer of electrons that surrounds the nucleus of an atom.
- **Inorganic:** Describes a substance that is not organic.
- **Insulator:** A substance that does not transfer an electric current or heat.
- **Nucleus:** The central core of an atom containing protons and neutrons.

NANOTUBES

Fullerenes do not have to be balls. In 1991, Japanese scientist Iijima Sumio (1939-) made fullerenes that were tube shaped. The tubes were made from a sheet of carbon atoms bonded in the same hexagon pattern as graphite molecules. The structures were named nanotubes. Nanotubes are very thin. One long enough to stretch from Earth to the Moon could be rolled into a ball the size of a poppy seed! So far, scientists can only make short pieces. If we learn how to make them long enough, there will be many uses for nanotubes. For example, the tubes could be woven to make a material many times stronger than steel, but much lighter.

because the electrons involved in the weak bonds break free easily. They then flow through the graphite crystal between the sheets of carbon atoms. All the electrons in diamond are held in strong bonds and cannot be released to form a current. As a result, diamond is an insulator.

Fullerenes

Fullerenes, the third structural form of carbon, are also conductors. However, the way their electrons are free to move is different again from other carbon allotropes. Looking at the structure of fullerenes will also help us understand the properties of organic compounds.

Fullerenes are made when carbon compounds are burned. These molecules are fragile, and in normal conditions they fall apart and form sootlike substances.

The smallest and simplest fullerene contains 60 carbon atoms. Its formula is C_{60}. This fullerene was the first to be discovered in 1985. It was named buckminsterfullerene for the designer of geodesic domes, which it closely resembles. All similar fragile carbon structures are now referred to as fullerenes, and C_{60} molecule has been nicknamed "the buckyball."

In a buckyball and other fullerenes, each carbon atom is bonded to three others. Most form into hexagons in the same way as in sheets of graphite. However, in a few cases they also form pentagons (five-sided shapes). This sheet of interconnected hexagons and pentagons curves into a sphere.

Unlike in diamond and graphite, the carbon atoms in fullerenes do not form a fourth bond. Instead, the spare, unbonded electrons from each atom are shared between them all. This creates a "cloud" of electrons that spreads evenly over the surface of the ball. The electrons in this cloud are free to move and carry an electric current.

It is hoped that fullerenes will be very useful substances. They have been made into nanotubes. Perhaps one day fullerenes will make pipes and wires in tiny machines. Fullerenes are hollow and can hold other atoms inside them. The atom inside is not bonded to the fullerene so the two do not form a compound. Chemists have had to come up with a new way of describing such arrangements. A helium atom (He) inside a buckyball is written as $He@C_{60}$.

A geodesic dome built by R. Buckminster Fuller in Montreal, Canada, in 1967, which resembles the shape of fullerenes.

BALLS OF FIRE

Diamond and graphite have been known about for thousands of years. However, a third form of carbon was discovered only 25 years ago. In 1985, English scientist Harold Kroto (1939–) teamed up with two U.S. chemists Richard Smalley (1943-2005) and Robert Curl (1933–). The trio were trying to figure out what the surface of a star might be like. They used a superhot laser to burn samples of carbon and then analyzed what was produced.

Their experiments produced a lot of clusters of carbon atoms, like the ones seen in soot. However, to their surprise they found that clusters containing 60 carbon atoms were also produced. These clusters were much bigger than they expected and did not break apart easily. The scientists realized that the carbon atoms must be forming a hollow, cagelike ball. Further experiments showed that balls and other hollow structures could be made with larger numbers of carbon atoms.

Kroto, Smalley, and Curl had discovered a new carbon allotrope and they won the Nobel Prize in Chemistry in 1996. They named the substances fullerenes after the U.S. architect R. Buckminster Fuller (1895-1983). In the 1950s, Fuller designed domes that, by chance, had the same shape and structure as the chemicals.

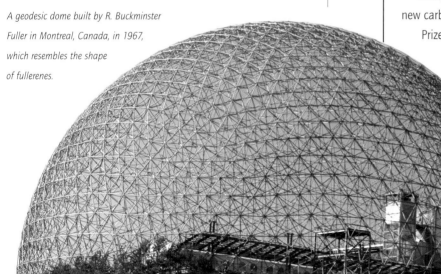

It is the ability of carbon atoms to form into chains that makes organic compounds so varied. There is no limit to the length of these chains, and they might branch into highly complex networks.

The simplest organic compounds contain just carbon (C) and hydrogen (H) atoms. These compounds are called hydrocarbons. Hydrocarbons occur mixed together in petroleum oil and natural gas. Gasoline and other fuels are examples of hydrocarbons. Hydrocarbons are also used to make thousands of other products.

Inside a hydrocarbon molecule, a carbon atom can be bonded to other carbon atoms or to hydrogen atoms. Each carbon atom is able to bond to up to four other atoms. A hydrogen atom can only form one bond. The hydrogen atoms in hydrocarbon molecules are always bonded to carbon atoms.

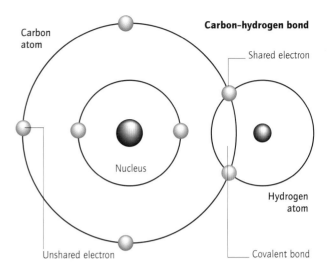

The covalent bond between a carbon and hydrogen atom.

SCIENCE WORDS

- **Alkane:** A hydrocarbon chain in which all atoms are connected by single bonds.
- **Chemical equation:** Symbols and numbers that show how reactants change into products during a reaction.
- **Combustion:** The reaction that causes burning. Combustion is generally a reaction with oxygen in the air.
- **Compound:** A substance formed when atoms of two or more different elements bond together.
- **Covalent bond:** A bond that forms between two or more atoms when they share electrons.
- **Hydrocarbon:** A type of organic compound containing only carbon and hydrogen atoms.
- **Molecule:** Two or more atoms that are connected together.

Strong bonds

Hydrocarbons are covalent compounds. The atoms are bonded because they are sharing electrons.

Carbon atoms can form into long chains because the bond between two carbon atoms is very stable. That is because carbon atoms have an outer electron shell that is half full.

The bond between a hydrogen and a carbon atom is also a strong one. Hydrogen atoms form stable bonds for the same reason that carbon atoms do. Hydrogen atoms have one electron shell. This shell can hold only two electrons, and hydrogen atoms have one. As a result, their electron shell is half full, just like in a carbon atom.

Hydrogen atoms can only form one bond each, so they cannot form chains. However, hydrogen forms the most complex and varied set of compounds in chemistry, when bonded with carbon.

Alkanes

The simplest hydrocarbon compounds are made of atoms connected by single bonds. This group of

Traffic runs along busy roads during an evening rush hour. Most automobiles and trucks are fueled with hydrocarbons, such as gasoline and diesel oil.

THE ALKANES

Alkane molecules are made using only single bonds. All carbon atoms in the molecules are bonded to the maximum of four other atoms. Many of the most familiar hydrocarbons are alkanes. Gasoline fuel contains a lot of octane (C_8H_{18}). Paraffin wax used to make candles is a mixture of alkane compounds each containing between 22 and 27 carbon atoms.

The three simplest alkanes:

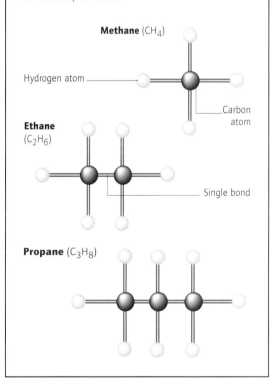

Methane (CH_4)

Hydrogen atom

Carbon atom

Ethane (C_2H_6)

Single bond

Propane (C_3H_8)

hydrocarbons is called the alkanes. Being made up of single bonds, alkane molecules have the same pyramid structure of diamond. However, the atoms form chains instead of a rigid network as in diamond. The shapes of alkanes and other organic compounds are complex, so all molecules are shown here as flat diagrams.

The smallest alkane is methane. This has the formula CH_4. A carbon atom is bonded to four hydrogen atoms. The next alkane is called ethane

(C_2H_6). It has two carbon atoms bonded together. Each carbon atom is attached to three hydrogen atoms. The next compound, propane (C_3H_8), has three carbons in a row, while butane (C_4H_{10}) has four.

Alkane molecules get larger by adding more carbon atoms. The compounds have the general formula $C_nH_{(2n+2)}$, where n is the number of carbon atoms in a molecule. For example, in methane n equals 1, so the number of hydrogen atoms is $(2 \times 1) + 2 = 4$.

Naming system

With so many compounds to understand, chemists have developed a system for naming organic compounds. They have agreed on a prefix (the beginning of a word)

THE ALKENES

A hydrocarbon containing carbon atoms that are joined by double bonds is called an alkene. The double bonds fix the shape of an alkene molecule. Single bonds allow sections of the molecule to spin around independently. The double bond cannot rotate so sections of the molecule cannot move. This has most effect on the structures of branched molecules, where branches are attached on certain sides of the double bond.

The two simplest alkenes:

Ethene (C_2H_4)

Carbon atom

Hydrogen atom

Propene (C_3H_6)

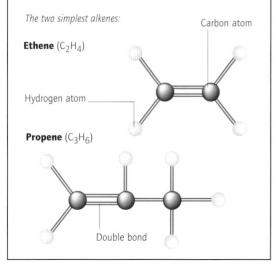

Double bond

---

for each number of carbon atoms in a molecule. For example, the prefix for two atoms is eth–, while molecules with eight atoms begin with oct–. All alkane compounds end in –ane. Therefore, C_2H_6 is called ethane and C_8H_{18} is named octane.

Alkane chemistry

As we have learned, the bonds in alkane molecules are very stable. As a result, alkane compounds are not very reactive. Their most important reaction is combustion, or burning. Combustion reactions occur when compounds react with oxygen (O).

When alkanes burn they release a lot of energy. That is why they make good fuels. For example, the natural gas extracted from underground is mainly methane. This gas is used in ovens, and boilers, and is also burned in power plants to make electricity.

The combustion reaction also produces carbon dioxide (CO_2) and water (H_2O). All hydrocarbons produce these when they burn, but different hydrocarbons produce them in different amounts. The equation for the combustion of methane is:

$$CH_4 + 2O_2 \rightarrow CO_2 + 2H_2O$$

Metalworkers use oxy-acetylene torches to cut metal. The acetylene (ethyne) burns with a very hot flame (5800–6300°F; 3200–3500°C) that melts steel. The oxygen then reacts with the melted steel to form iron oxide, which melts at a much lower temperature.

Alkenes

In an alkane, each carbon atom has four single bonds. Chemists say that alkanes are saturated hydrocarbons: the atoms inside are all bonded to the maximum number of other atoms. A molecule that contains carbon atoms that are bonded to fewer than four other atoms is described as being unsaturated.

Hydrocarbons that contain carbon atoms bonded to just three other atoms are called alkenes. The simplest alkene is ethene (C_2H_4). In a molecule of ethene, the two carbon atoms are connected by a double bond. With two bonds used up connecting to the other atom, some of the carbon atoms have just two bonds left for hydrogen atoms.

The alkenes increase in size in the same way as the alkanes: propene (C_3H_6) contains three carbon atoms and butene (C_4H_8) contains four. As with the alkanes, there is no limit to the length of an alkene chain.

Alkene chemistry

Alkenes occur in petroleum mixed in with alkanes and other hydrocarbons. However, people also make alkenes because the double bonds make alkenes useful. Whereas alkanes are just burned as fuel, alkenes can be reacted with other compounds to make many products.

Alkenes are reactive because a double bond readily breaks to form two single bonds. For example, alkenes will react with hydrogen gas (H_2) to become alkanes. The reaction that turns ethene into ethane has the following equation:

$$C_2H_4 + H_2 \rightarrow C_2H_6$$

This reaction is called an addition reaction because hydrogen has been added to the molecule.

Alkynes

Hydrocarbons that contain triple bonds between two carbon atoms are called alkynes. This group of compounds is more reactive than the alkenes. That is because a triple bond breaks to form three single bonds even more easily than a double bond breaks. Alkynes are so reactive they are not very common in

---

THE ALKYNES

Alkynes are hydrocarbons that have carbon atoms connected to each other by triple bonds. In the simplest alkyne, ethyne, each carbon atom is bonded to just one hydrogen atom. Larger alkyne molecules do not have triple bonds between all the carbon atoms. Just one triple bond is enough to make them alkynes.

Ethyne (C_2H_2)

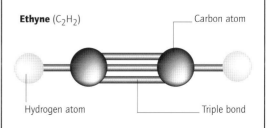

Carbon atom

Hydrogen atom

Triple bond

petroleum oil. They are made in laboratories instead. The simplest alkyne is ethyne (C_2H_2), also called acetylene.

Like the alkenes, alkynes are used to make useful chemicals, such as plastics and medicines. Ethyne is also used in torches for welding and cutting metal.

Petrochemicals

Before hydrocarbons such as alkanes and alkenes can be used for fuels or in industry, they must be refined. Refined hydrocarbons are called petrochemicals.

The main source of hydrocarbons is petroleum. This is a mixture of gases, liquids, and sludgelike solids. The word petroleum comes from the two Latin words for "rock" and "oil." Most petroleum is deep underground and it must be pumped to the surface. Petroleum is the remains of life-forms that have become buried under rocks over millions of years.

OIL SPILLS

Every day the world uses 85 million barrels of oil. One barrel of oil contains 42 gallons (159 l). That adds up to 150 million gallons an hour! All this oil needs to reach refineries. Most of the oil is taken in giant ships called tankers.

The largest tankers carry 400,000 tons (360 t) of oil. What happens when a tanker spills its oil? Crude oil floats on water forming a "slick." Sometimes the gasoline and other fuels catch fire. If the slick can be kept together out at sea with long booms, it can be cleared up. Oil that washes onto the coast and into the mouths of rivers will kill fish, birds, and other wildlife and takes months to clear away.

Fractions

Unrefined petroleum is called crude oil. Once at a refinery, any gases, water, and unwanted solids, such as mud, are removed. The hydrocarbons that remain are then pumped into the bottom of a tall tower and heated to 720°F (380°C).

The tower is a fractional distillation column. It is used to separate the different sizes, or fractions, of hydrocarbon molecules. Heating the petroleum makes most of the hydrocarbons boil and turn into a gas.

The mixture of gases flows up the column. As the gas rises, it begins to cool down and turn into liquids. These liquids are collected at several points inside the column. Small and light hydrocarbon molecules, such as pentane (C_5H_{12}), have lower boiling points than large and heavy ones. The light molecules stay as gases until they get to the top of the column, where they are collected. Heavier fractions turn to liquid at points lower down, where they are collected.

Breaking the chains

Most of the hydrocarbons in crude oil are alkanes with straight chains. Around 90 percent of crude oil ends

Because oil is lighter than water, it floats on the surface of the sea. It coats everything that the water touches, including land and animals.

up as fuel—mainly gasoline for cars. However, after the fractions have been separated, only about 20 percent of them are useful immediately. The rest are pumped into chambers called reactors, where they are converted into more useful molecules.

Inside the reactors, the hydrocarbons are "cracked." Cracking is a process that breaks long alkane molecules into shorter alkanes and alkenes. Cracking requires the hydrocarbons to be very hot and under high pressure, but that alone is not enough. Cracking reactions require catalysts. A catalyst is a substance that helps a reaction along, but is not changed after the reaction has finished.

The catalysts used in cracking are zeolites. These are very complex hollow structures made from aluminum and silicon compounds. The hydrocarbons crack into smaller molecules as they are pumped through the zeolites.

Good gasoline

The cracked hydrocarbons are then separated into fractions in the same way as before. Again only some of the products are useful as fuel. This time the unwanted molecules are too small and light to be used in gasoline.

The best hydrocarbons for gasoline are small, branched alkanes. They burn more slowly than unbranched compounds and keep an engine running smoothly.

Another process, called alkylation, converts the small, light alkanes and alkenes produced by cracking into larger branched alkanes. The catalysts used in alkylation are strong acids.

Coal

Crude oil is not the only source of hydrocarbons. Coal is a rock made from pure carbon mixed with hydrocarbons. Coal is used as a fuel and is reacted with ores to make pure metals. In the past, coal was a source of a fuel called coal gas. This gas is poisonous and has been replaced with natural gas.

BRANCHED MOLECULES

Not all hydrocarbons are straight chains. Molecules with four or more carbon atoms can divide into branches. A branched molecule may contain the same number of atoms as a straight molecule, and their chemical formulas will be the same. Chemists use the naming system to describe how each molecule is organized instead.

A molecule's name is determined by the size of its longest straight chain. Alkane 1 (below) has four carbon atoms in a single chain. It is therefore named butane.

Alkane 1

Butane
(C_4H_{10})

Alkane 2 also has four carbon atoms. However, its longest chain has three carbon atoms (like propane). The other carbon and its three hydrogen atoms ($-CH_3$, or methyl) are attached to the middle of the chain. The molecule is named methyl propane.

Alkane 2

Methyl propane

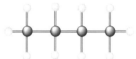
Methyl group ($-CH_3$)

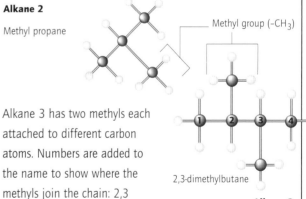
2,3-dimethylbutane

Alkane 3

Alkane 3 has two methyls each attached to different carbon atoms. Numbers are added to the name to show where the methyls join the chain: 2,3 dimethylbutane. Methyls and other branches are called alkyl groups. Their names are based on the number of carbon atoms they contain:

Number of carbons	Alkyl group	Formula
1	Methyl-	$-CH_3$
2	Ethyl-	$-C_2H_5$
3	Propyl-	$-C_3H_7$
4	Butyl-	$-C_4H_9$

CARBON RINGS

As well as forming chains, hydrocarbon compounds can also form rings. Many of these ringed molecules have unusual chemical properties.

Hydrocarbon molecules that form chains follow a structure that is similar to that of diamond. Like in a diamond crystal, the carbon and hydrogen atoms form into a series of pyramid structures. However, there are hydrocarbons with structures that are more similar to graphite.

Like diamond, graphite is a form of pure carbon. Instead of forming pyramids, the atoms in graphite form hexagons, or six-sided rings. Hydrocarbon

THE BENZENE RING

Benzene (C_6H_6) is the simplest arene. Its six carbon atoms form a ring. They are connected to each other by three single and three double bonds. The position of these bonds is not fixed. The double bonds and single bonds can swap places. As a result, the molecule's three double bonds become shared between all six of the carbon atoms.

Two ways of showing the structure of benzene:

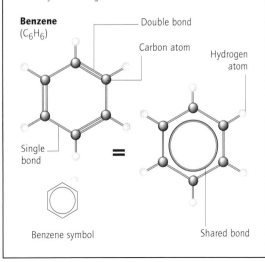

Benzene (C_6H_6)
Double bond
Carbon atom
Hydrogen atom
Single bond
Shared bond
Benzene symbol

BONDS IN BENZENE AND DELOCALIZED ELECTRONS

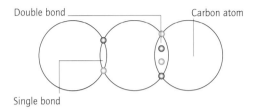

Double bond
Carbon atom
Single bond

Three carbon atoms are connected by a single and double bond.

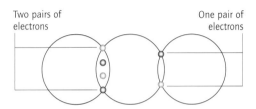

Two pairs of electrons
One pair of electrons

The positions of the single and double bond can swap sides.

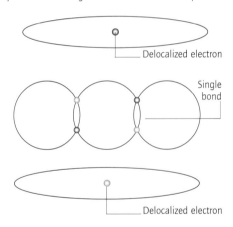

Delocalized electron
Single bond
Delocalized electron

The second pair of electrons from the double bond becomes delocalized and shared by all the atoms.

molecules that contain similar hexagons are called arenes. Another name for them is aromatic compounds, because many of them have a strong aroma (odor).

Benzene

The simplest arene is a compound called benzene. A benzene molecule contains six carbon (C) atoms and six hydrogen (H) atoms. The compound's chemical formula is C_6H_6.

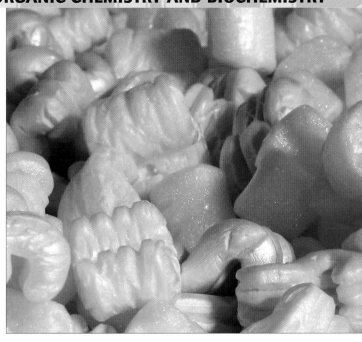

Pieces of styrofoam are made from a plastic called polystyrene that has been pumped full of air. Polystyrene is made up of many ringed molecules joined together.

The six carbon atoms are connected into a hexagon. Each carbon atom is also bonded to a single hydrogen atom. Carbon atoms form a total of four bonds. In benzene, the carbon atoms are connected to just three other atoms. Thus, each carbon atom forms a double bond with one of its neighboring carbon atoms. As a result, the hexagon of atoms is held together with a mixture of single and double bonds. The two types of bonds are arranged alternately.

Sharing electrons

The bonds in a molecule of benzene are covalent. A covalent bond forms between atoms that are sharing electrons. The single bonds in the benzene molecule form when two carbon atoms share a pair of electrons. The double bonds form when two atoms share two pairs of electrons (see diagram left).

The two pairs of electrons in a double bond are not the same. The first pair forms in the same way as a pair in a single bond. The second pair of electrons are held together less strongly. They are more likely to break apart and form a bond with another atom.

In a benzene ring, each of the carbon atoms has formed a single and a double bond with the two carbon atoms on either side. Because the carbon atoms are connected in a ring, they all form a single bond on one side, and a double bond on the other. However, one pair of electrons can move from one side of the carbon atom to the other. As it does this, the double bond becomes a single bond, while the single bond becomes a double. As a result, that pair of electrons is effectively shared between the bonds on

---

ARENE COMPOUNDS

An arene is any compound that contains one or more benzenelike rings in its molecule. Arene compounds may have a chain of carbon atoms (an alkyl group) branching out from the ring in place of a hydrogen atom. Other arene molecules contain two or more joined rings.

Naphthalene $C_{10}H_8$

Xylene $C_6H_4(CH_3)_2$

$-CH_3$ (methyl)

Xylene symbol

Toluene $C_6H_4CH_3$

Toluene symbol

Naphthalene symbol

AZO DYES

Many of the dyes used to color our clothes are aromatic compounds. These compounds are called azo dyes because they contain a section in the molecule called an azo group. An azo group is formed when one part of a hydrocarbon is connected to another section by two nitrogen (N) atoms. The nitrogen atoms sit between the two parts of the molecule and are connected to each other by a double bond.

Azo groups can form in chained hydrocarbons, but these compounds are very unstable. However, when an azo group attaches to a benzene ring, it forms a stable molecule. The double bond between the nitrogen atoms becomes part of the benzene's system of delocalized electrons. That keeps the molecule stable.

Many azo compounds are brightly colored, mostly red, orange, or yellow. Azo dyes were first used in the 1880s. The first was called Congo red. However, this and other early dyes have been replaced with other azo dyes, which last longer. Most azo dyes are poisonous, but some, such as tartrazine yellow, are used to color food.

---

both sides of the atom. Because the carbon atoms form a ring, their double bonds fuse into a single shared bond.

The electrons inside this shared bond are described as delocalized. They are not linked to one bond, but shared between the bonds connecting several atoms.

Stable molecules

All arenes contain rings held together with delocalized electrons. Some arene compounds have a single ring with chained sections attached to them. Other arenes are made up of several rings joined together.

The delocalized electrons make the molecules of benzene and other arenes more stable than many other hydrocarbons. Chemists measure how strongly the atoms in a molecule are bonded to each other by measuring how much heat is released when the compound burns.

Burning is a reaction between a compound and oxygen (O_2). During the reaction, the compound breaks apart and its atoms bond with oxygen atoms. The heat released during burning is the energy left over after the old molecules have broken apart and formed into new ones. More stable hydrocarbons release less heat when they burn, because more of the energy has been used up breaking the strong bonds in their molecules.

Chemists can measure how strong a single bond between two carbon atoms is by burning simple alkanes. They can also test the strength of a double bond by burning an alkene.

Chemists could then add these values together to figure out how strong the three single and three double bonds are in a ring of benzene. However, when

Mothballs are made from naphthalene, an arene compound. The smell keeps moths away, and prevents caterpillars from eating holes in clothing.

this result is tested by burning benzene in a laboratory, chemists find that the molecule's bonds are stronger than they thought. The delocalized electrons are shared equally among all the bonds, making them all stronger.

Arene chemistry

The stability of the delocalized electrons has an effect on the way benzene and other arenes react. Hydrocarbons with double bonds in their molecules tend to be reactive. That is because the double bond easily breaks to form two single bonds. For example, an alkene will react with hydrogen (H_2) to become an alkane. In this reaction, the alkene's double bond breaks and forms single bonds with hydrogen atoms.

That sort of reaction is called an addition, because the hydrogen atoms are added to the molecule. With three double bonds in its molecule, benzene might also be expected to be reactive in that way. However, benzene and other arenes do not take part in addition reactions with hydrogen. The delocalized electrons stop the molecule's double bonds from breaking and forming into single bonds.

Instead, arenes undergo displacement reactions, where an atom or molecule takes the place of one of the hydrogen atoms. Only very reactive elements, such as the halogens, will react with arenes in this way. For example, chlorine (Cl_2) reacts with benzene (C_6H_6) to

SCIENCE WORDS

- **Atom:** The smallest piece of an element that still retains the properties of that element.
- **Compound:** A substance formed when atoms of two or more different elements bond together.
- **Hydrocarbon:** A type of organic compound containing only atoms of the elements carbon (C) and hydrogen (H).
- **Molecule:** Two or more atoms connected by chemical bonds.

MAKING A BANG

One of the most familiar and common explosives is an arene compound. Most people have heard of TNT. These letters stand for trinitrotoluene. TNT is used in bombs, to demolish old buildings, and to blast away rocks in mines.

Toluene is an arene compound. It is a benzene ring with a methyl group ($-CH_3$) attached. A molecule of TNT is a toluene molecule that also has three nitro groups ($-NO_2$) attached.

When it explodes, TNT is very powerful. However, it is also relatively stable. It does not react easily and stays safe when it gets hot or wet. TNT will explode if a detonator is used to make it hot enough to react; that is 563°F (295°C). At this temperature the molecules of TNT break apart, and the nitro groups react with each other to make gases. These gases expand very rapidly and cause a shockwave in the air. It is this shockwave that causes damage to solid objects in its path.

The power of large explosions is measured in kilotons. A 1-kiloton explosion releases the same amount of energy as an explosion of 1,000 tons (907 t) of TNT.

make chlorobenzene (C_6H_5Cl) and hydrochloric acid (HCl). The chemical equation for this reaction is:

$$C_6H_6 + Cl_2 \rightarrow C_6H_5Cl + HCl$$

Poisons and cures

Benzene and several other arene compounds are very poisonous. Even a tiny amount of benzene in food or water is enough to make a person ill. Benzene damages the body's immune system and nerves and causes cancer. However, many life-saving medicines and painkillers are also arene compounds.

ALCOHOLS AND ACIDS

Not all organic compounds are hydrocarbons. Many of them contain atoms of other elements. Oxygen is a common ingredient in organic compounds. These compounds include alcohols and organic acids, such as vinegar.

Hydrocarbons are compounds that contain just carbon (C) and hydrogen (H) atoms. As we have seen, the bonds between atoms of these elements are very strong and unlikely to break. As a result, hydrocarbons are not very reactive. However, when atoms of other elements are added to the compounds, they become more reactive. That is because the bonds between the carbon atoms and these other atoms are much weaker and more likely to break open and take part in a chemical reaction.

The section of an organic molecule that contains an atom that is not carbon or hydrogen is called a functional group. The structure of a functional group determines how that compound will react with other chemicals.

Adding oxygen

Oxygen (O) forms a number of functional groups in organic compounds. An oxygen atom can form a total of two bonds with other atoms. For example, water is a compound of oxygen and hydrogen. One oxygen atom is bonded to two hydrogen atoms to make the molecule H_2O. Imagine if one of the hydrogen atoms was

Alcoholic drinks, such as wine and beer, are made using a natural process called fermentation. Ethanol (C_2H_5OH) is produced by fermenting glucose, a sugar ($C_6H_{12}O_6$). The reaction also produces carbon dioxide (CO_2). Fermentation occurs inside living cells. The reaction releases energy.

replaced with a carbon atom in a hydrocarbon molecule. That hydrocarbon would then have an oxygen atom and a hydrogen atom (–OH) attached to it. This –OH structure is a functional group called a hydroxyl. Organic chain compounds with a hydroxyl group belong to the group of compounds called the alcohols. Hydroxyl groups on an arene compound form compounds called phenols.

Making alcohols

Alcohols are some of the most familiar organic compounds. They occur naturally, and people have been making them for thousands of years.

The most common alcohol compound is ethanol (C_2H_5OH). Ethanol is often called grain alcohol because it can be made from sugars in grain and fruits. This occurs through a series of reactions called fermentation.

Fermentation reactions involve sugar reacting with oxygen. They occur in nature, and they are used to make alcoholic beverages.

The other common type of alcohol is methanol (CH_3OH). This compound is sometimes called wood alcohol because it can be made by heating wood. If the wood is kept out of the air so it does not burn, it will produce methanol vapors.

Methanol is poisonous, just like all alcohols. Only ethanol can be consumed in small quantities. But in large amounts even ethanol can kill, which is known as alcohol poisoning. Most of the simple alcohols are used as solvents.

Alcohol molecules that have two hydroxyl groups in their molecules are called glycols. A few compounds have even more hydroxyl groups. For example, glycerol–$C_3H_5(OH)_3$–has three hydroxyl groups.

Uneven charges

Oxygen atoms are very reactive. They pull on electrons more strongly than the atoms of most other elements do. The oxygen atom in an alcohol molecule pulls electrons away from the carbon and hydrogen atoms nearby. As a result, the oxygen atom becomes slightly negatively charged. The hydrogen bonded to it has a slight positive charge. Opposite charges attract each other, so the hydrogen atom on one alcohol molecule is drawn toward the oxygen atom on the other. That creates a weak bond between the two molecules. This attraction is called a hydrogen bond. Many oxygen compounds form hydrogen bonds, including water.

Hydrogen bonds hold alcohol molecules together more strongly. As a result, the boiling points of alcohols are higher than those of hydrocarbons without oxygen. The boiling point is the temperature at which the molecules in a liquid break free of each other and turn into a gas. Both methanol and ethanol are liquids in normal conditions. Without hydrogen bonds between their molecules, these alcohols would be gases.

The negative charge of the oxygen atom also affects the way alcohols react. For example, they react with oxygen to make compounds called aldehydes and ketones. Alcohols will also react with oxygen to form acidic compounds called carboxylic acids.

ALCOHOLS

When a hydroxyl group (-OH) containing an oxygen and hydrogen atom joins to a hydrocarbon chain, it forms a compound called an alcohol. Alcohols are named according to the number of carbons in their molecules. Their names generally end in -ol.

Three simple alcohol compounds:

Methanol (CH_3OH)

Ethanol (C_2H_5OH)

Propanol (C_3H_7OH)

Hydroxyl group (-OH)

Single bond

Carbon atom

Oxygen atom

Hydrogen atom

Carboxylic acids

Carboxylic acids have two functional groups. One of them is a hydroxyl (–OH), the group also found in alcohols and phenols. The other functional group is called a carbonyl (–CO). In this group, an oxygen atom is bonded to a carbon atom. The two atoms are connected by a double bond.

In a carboxylic acid molecule, both of these functional groups are attached to the same carbon atom. Together they form a carboxyl group (–COOH).

Common acids

Just like the alcohols and other organic compounds, carboxylic acids are named according to how many carbon atoms there are in their molecules. All their names end in -oic.

However, many carboxylic acids are found in foods or occur elsewhere in nature, and over the years they

ANTISEPTICS

Today, a surgeon's operating room is very clean. No one is allowed in unless they wash themselves and put on protective clothing. If any dirt got into a patient's body during an operation, then he or she might become very ill and die. The dirt contains tiny life-forms called bacteria, which infect the body and cause illness.

About 150 years ago, people did not understand these risks. People often died after operations, not because of the surgery itself, but because of infections. In 1865, a British surgeon named Joseph Lister (1827-1912) began using carbolic acid (phenol in water) to make operating rooms sterile (free of bacteria). The phenol was acidic enough to kill bacteria, but it was also mild so it did not hurt the patient. Lister's idea led to the way surgery is performed today.

SCIENCE WORDS

- **Acid:** A compound that splits easily into a positively charged hydrogen ion and another negatively charged ion.
- **Benzene:** A ring of carbon atoms in which some electrons are shared by all atoms in the molecule.
- **Carbonyl:** A functional group in which an oxygen atom is connected to a carbon atom by a double bond.
- **Ion:** An atom or molecule that has lost or gained one or more electrons and has become electrically charged.

Formic acid, from the Latin word for ant (formica), was discovered as an acidic vapor that rises from anthills. It is found in ant stings.

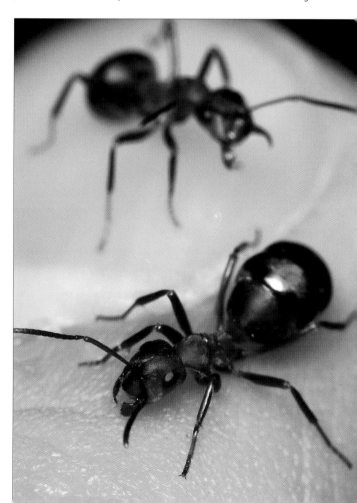

CARBOXYLIC ACIDS

The main group of organic acids are called the carboxylic acids. They have a hydroxyl (-OH) and carbonyl (-CO) group bonded together. Some carboxylic acids have several of these groups.

Carboxylic acids split into ions. A hydrogen ion (H^+) breaks away from the rest of the molecule, which becomes a negatively charged carboxylate ion. For example, methanoic acid forms methanoate ions ($HCOO^-$).

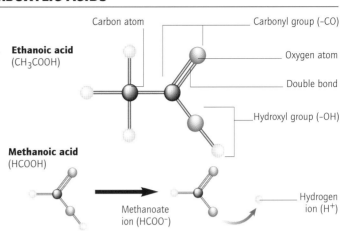

Ethanoic acid (CH_3COOH)

Carbon atom — Carbonyl group (-CO)

Oxygen atom

Double bond

Hydroxyl group (-OH)

Methanoic acid ($HCOOH$)

Methanoate ion ($HCOO^-$)

Hydrogen ion (H^+)

have been given other names. For example, vinegar contains ethanoic acid (CH_3COOH). This compound is also known as acetic acid. Methanoic acid ($HCOOH$) is known as formic acid, which is present in insect bites and stings, particularly ants.

There are many other natural carboxylic acids. These include citric acid from lemons, oranges, and other citrus fruits. Lactic acid is made by muscles when they work hard. It is this acid reacting with other compounds in the muscles that makes them ache and feel tired.

Longer carboxylic acid molecules are called fatty acids. They are found in milk, oils, and fats. For example, lauric acid occurs in coconut milk.

Acid reactions

Carboxylic acids are made when alcohols react with oxygen (O_2). Ethanoic acid is made in nature as part of the same fermentation process that turns sugars into ethanol (C_2H_5OH). As we have seen, yeast makes the alcohol, but the changes do not end there. If the ethanol is exposed to the air, bacteria mixed into it will turn it into ethanoic acid. This reaction has the following equation:

$$C_2H_5OH + O_2 \rightarrow CH_3COOH + H_2O$$

That is why wine and other alcoholic beverages will begin to taste sour after being opened for a long time. They are slowly turning into vinegar!

Positively charged hydrogen ions (H^+) break off carboxylic acid molecules. That is why they are classed as acids. Acids are reactive compounds because they produce hydrogen ions. Acids react with other compounds to produce substances called salts.

When it loses its hydrogen ion, the rest of the carboxylic acid becomes a negatively charged ion. During a reaction, this ion forms a salt. The salts of carboxylic acids have names ending in -oate.

When ethanoic acid (CH_3COOH) reacts with calcium hydroxide, $Ca(OH)_3$, it produces water (H_2O) and calcium ethanoate, $Ca(CH_3COO)_2$. The equation for this reaction looks like this:

$$2CH_3COOH + Ca(OH)_2 \rightarrow$$
$$Ca(CH_3COO)_2 + H_2O$$

Food can be stored for a long time by pickling. Food is pickled in either vinegar (ethanoic acid) or strong alcohol (ethanol). The acid in vinegar stops bacteria on the food from growing. Food that has bacteria growing on it will go bad. The vinegar also soaks into the food giving it a strong flavor.

There are many types of functional groups, and each one gives organic compounds certain properties. As well as containing oxygen atoms, there are also functional groups that contain atoms of other elements.

There are many classes of organic compounds. A compound is formed when atoms of two or more elements bond together. Organic compounds are made up of mostly atoms of carbon (C) and hydrogen (H). Compounds containing only these elements are known

as hydrocarbons. However, many organic molecules also contain atoms of other elements. Where these atoms bond to the hydrocarbon, they form a functional group. The functional group has an effect on the way that compound behaves.

Acid plus alcohol

As we have seen, alcohol and carboxylic acids are types of organic compounds that are common in the natural world. They both have functional groups containing oxygen.

When an alcohol and carboxylic acid react, they form a compound called an ester. An ester forms when an alcohol's functional group reacts with the functional group of the acid. Alcohols have a hydroxyl functional group made from an oxygen and hydrogen atom (-OH). Carboxylic acids have a hydroxyl group, too, but they also have a carbonyl group. That is a carbon atom connected to an oxygen atom by a double bond.

To make an ester, the alcohol loses a hydrogen atom from its hydroxyl group. The oxygen atom left behind attaches to the carbon atom in the acid's

ESTERS

When alcohols react with carboxylic acids they form compounds called esters. An ester molecule has two halves, one side coming from the alcohol and the other from the acid. These two sections are connected by an oxygen atom. The side of the molecule that was originally from the acid contains a carbonyl group (-CO).

Two simple ester molecules:

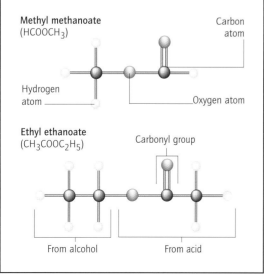

Methyl methanoate
($HCOOCH_3$)

Carbon atom

Hydrogen atom

Oxygen atom

Ethyl ethanoate
($CH_3COOC_2H_5$)

Carbonyl group

From alcohol

From acid

methanoate. One side comes from the methanol. That has lost a hydrogen atom and becomes the methyl part of the ester. The section from the methanoic acid has lost its hydroxyl group. The section produced by that is called methanoate.

Odors and oils

Most small ester compounds are liquids. These liquids evaporate easily (turn into a gas), and many of them have a distinctive smell.

Large ester compounds do not evaporate easily. Instead they are oily liquids and waxy solids. Some animal fats and vegetable oils are complex ester compounds. Such fats and oils are made up of three carboxylic acid molecules connected to an alcohol

Many of nature's smells and tastes, such as the pleasant fragrance of flowers (above), are produced by organic compounds. Compounds containing nitrogen or sulfur, give the foul odor of the cuckoo pint (right).

carbonyl group. The acid also loses its hydroxyl to form an ester. The hydroxyl group and hydrogen atom also bond together to make water (H_2O).

Like all organic compounds, esters are named according to how many carbon atoms they have. The simplest ester is methyl methanoate ($HCOOCH_3$). This compound is produced when methanol (CH_3OH) reacts with methanoic acid ($HCOOH$; also called formic acid). The equation for the reaction is:

$$HCOOH + CH_3OH \rightarrow HCOOCH_3 + H_2O$$

The ester's name has two parts because its molecule is in two parts. The ester is named methyl

---

SCIENCE WORDS

- **Aldehyde:** A compound with a carbonyl group attached to the end of its molecule.
- **Carbonyl:** A functional group made by a carbon atom connected to an oxygen atom by a double bond.
- **Compound:** Atoms of different elements bonded together.
- **Ester:** A compound formed when an alcohol reacts with a carboxylic acid.
- **Ether:** Compound in which two hydrocarbon groups are joined by an oxygen atom.
- **Evaporate:** To turn from liquid to gas.
- **Functional group:** A section of an organic molecule that gives it certain chemical properties.
- **Ketone:** A compound with a carbonyl group attached in the middle of its molecule.
- **Molecule:** Two or more atoms that are connected together.
- **Organic:** Describes a compound that is made of carbon and that generally also contains hydrogen.

called glycerol. Glycerol molecules have three hydroxyl groups (–OH), and each one forms an ester with a large carboxylic acid, known as a fatty acid. Fatty acids may be saturated or unsaturated. Saturated molecules contain only single bonds, while unsaturated molecules have one or more double bonds. Most animal fats are saturated compounds; many vegetable oils are unsaturated fatty acids.

Aldehydes and ketones

There are two classes of organic compounds that have a single carbonyl (–CO) as their functional group. They are the aldehydes and ketones. Both classes of compounds are very similar. The only difference in their structures is that an aldehyde has a carbonyl group attached to the end of its molecule. A ketone has the same group attached in the middle of the molecule. These compounds are classed as two groups because the difference in their structure has an effect on their reactivity.

The names of aldehydes and ketones are based on how many carbon atoms they contain. Aldehydes have names that end in –al, while ketones have names ending in –one.

The simplest aldehyde is methanal (H_2CO). This compound is perhaps more familiar by its old name, formaldehyde. The simplest ketone is propanone

---

AMINES

An amine is an organic compound containing a nitrogen atom. Amines are similar to ammonia (NH_3). An amine compound has hydrocarbons in place of at least one of the hydrogen atoms. Amines are reactive compounds. They are used to make certain dyes.

A molecule of methylamine, the simplest amine compound.

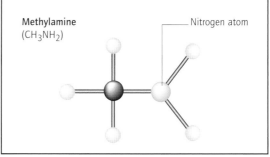

Methylamine (CH_3NH_2)

Nitrogen atom

(CH_3COCH_3). Again, this compound is also commonly referred to by its older name, acetone.

Carbonyl chemistry

Aldehydes and ketones are more reactive than most organic compounds because of the carbonyl group. The double bond holding the oxygen to the compound is

---

ALDEHYDES

There are two types of compounds that have just a carbonyl as their functional group. Aldehydes have this carbonyl at the end of each molecule. Ketones have carbonyls in the middle of each molecule. The carbonyl group is made up of an oxygen connected to a carbon atom by a double bond. It is a very reactive functional group.

The two simplest aldehyde compounds:

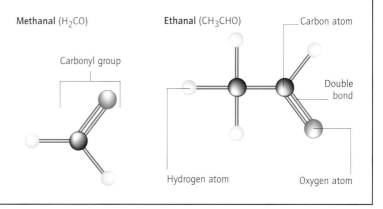

Methanal (H_2CO)

Carbonyl group

Ethanal (CH_3CHO)

Carbon atom

Double bond

Hydrogen atom

Oxygen atom

very likely to break and form two single bonds. The oxygen atom pulls the electrons away from the carbon atom and gains a slight negative charge. Other molecules are attracted to this negative charge, which is why the oxygen atom is so likely to be involved in a reaction.

Aldehydes and ketones are halfway between alcohols and carboxylic acids. An alcohol can become an aldehyde or ketone by losing two hydrogen atoms. For example, methanol (CH_3OH) becomes methanal (H_2CO) through the reaction:

$$CH_3OH \rightarrow H_2CO + H_2$$

Ethers

An organic compound that has an oxygen atom bonded between two carbon atoms is called an ether. Ethers are made when two alcohols join together. During this reaction, two hydrogen atoms (H_2) and an oxygen atom (O) are taken from the alcohol molecules and become a molecule of water (H_2O). The reaction is described as a dehydration because water is being removed from the alcohols as they are joined together.

Because their oxygen atoms are bonded strongly to two carbons atoms, ethers are not very reactive. However, ethoxyethane ($C_2H_5OC_2H_5$) was used as the first anesthetic.

KETONES

The simplest ketone has three carbon atoms. That is because a ketone has to have its carbonyl group located in the middle of the molecule. Apart from propanone, other ketones have numbers in their names. These numbers show which carbon atom the carbonyl group is attached to.

A molecule of propanone.

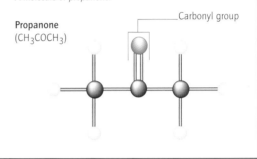

Propanone (CH_3COCH_3)

Carbonyl group

Nitrogen group

An organic compound that contains a single nitrogen atom (N) is called an amine. Nitrogen atoms can form three bonds. In an amine, all of them are single bonds.

The nitrogen atom sits at the center of the molecule, which is in three sections. In a simple amine, two of those sections might simply be hydrogen atoms. At least one of the sections is an alkyl group. An alkyl group is a section of hydrocarbon that branches off another molecule or is attached to a functional group. For example, the simplest alkyl group is a methyl ($-CH_3$). So the simplest amine is called methylamine (CH_3NH_2).

The nitrogen atom may be bonded to two alkyl groups, for example, a methyl and an ethyl ($-C_2H_5$). In this case, the alkyl groups are listed alphabetically, so the molecule is named ethylmethylamine. When there are two methyl groups, it is dimethylamine; if there are three, then the name is trimethylamine.

Methoxymethane is used to make the spray in aerosol cans.

POLYMERS

Polymers are compounds made from long chains of smaller molecules. Polymers occur naturally in the world around us. They are also made from petrochemicals for use as plastics and to make clothing.

NATURAL POLYMERS

Nature is full of polymers. The bodies of plants, such as the wood inside trees, are made from a polymer called cellulose. This compound is a chain of sugar monomers. Starch is another polymer made from sugars. It is the soft material in bread, potatoes, and rice.

Even genes, the coded instructions that control how living bodies grow, are a polymer. That polymer is called deoxyribonucleic acid (DNA). It is made using four monomers. Each gene is coded with a unique combination of these monomers.

Rubber is also a natural polymer. It comes from latex, the sticky white sap of the rubber tree. Adding acid and salt separates the solid polymer from the liquid part of the sap. At this stage raw rubber is soft and stringy, like the cheese on a pizza. A process called vulcanization makes the rubber much tougher and harder.

Latex is tapped from a rubber tree. Rubber made from latex is now often replaced with similar polymers made from hydrocarbons.

The world's main source of hydrocarbons is petroleum, or crude oil. Nine-tenths of the hydrocarbons in crude oil are turned into gasoline and other fuels.

What happens to the rest? Most of it is turned into compounds called polymers. Polymers are as varied as they are useful. They are used in everything from fighter planes to frying pans.

Chains of molecules

Polymers are very large molecules. They are made up of many smaller molecules that are connected into a chain. The smaller units are called monomers. The word *mono* means "alone," while *poly* means "many." So, a polymer is a compound that contains many monomers. Monomers form polymers in a process called polymerization.

Types of polymers

There are many types of polymers. Some occur in nature, but people make most of the polymers around us from petrochemicals. Many polymers are known as plastics. They can be molded into any shape. Other

Left: Plastic balls are made from polymers. Polymers can be made into any shape and are used in place of all types of naturally-occurring materials, such as wood, stone, glass, china, and metals.

polymers are called rubbers. They are stretchy, or elastic, and can be bent out of shape easily, but always spring back to their original form.

The properties of polymers are determined by their monomers and the way the chains are formed.

Making polymers

Monomers can be made to polymerize (form into a polymer) through a number of reactions. Monomers that have double bonds, such as alkenes, are

MONOMERS

Polymers are chains of smaller molecules called monomers. A polymer may be made up of just one type of monomer. Such polymers are called homopolymers. (The word *homo* means "same.") Other polymers contain two or more types of monomers that are bonded alternately, one after the other. These polymers are called copolymers. (The word *co* means "together.")

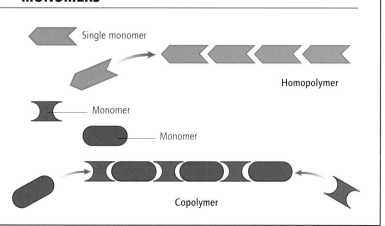

Single monomer

Homopolymer

Monomer

Monomer

Copolymer

WHAT ARE PLASTICS?

People use most of the polymers discussed in this chapter to make plastics. Plastics are very useful materials because they can be made into any shape. The word *plastic* comes from the Greek word for "mold."

Plastics have many advantages over other materials. For example, plastics do not rust or corrode like metals. They can be made to be flexible, so they do not shatter like glass. They are also waterproof, unlike wood. Plastics are also good insulators—they do not carry an electric current. Electric cables are coated in plastic to make them safe to handle.

A few rubberlike natural polymers can be made into plastic, but plastics are really human-made materials. The first plastics were invented in the late 19th century. These early plastics were brittle (shattered easily) and expensive to make, so they were not used as widely as plastics are today. Plastics today are very inexpensive and are used in everything from spacecraft to shopping bags.

There are two types of plastics: thermoplastics and thermosets. The word *thermo* means "heat." A thermoplastic becomes softer and more moldable when it gets hot. It eventually melts and can be remolded into any shape. Polyethylene and PVC are thermoplastics.

A thermoset is the opposite of a thermoplastic. It gets harder as it is heated. Once it has hardened, a thermoset will not melt. Thermosets are molded into objects that need to stay rigid when hot. Polyester and rubber are thermosets.

Modern polymers versus traditional materials

Application	Polymer	Traditional material	Advantages of polymer
Molded objects	Polypropene	Metal	This plastic is rigid like metal, but much lighter. It can also be molded at lower temperatures.
Bottles	PET (Polyethylene terephthalate)	Glass	PET is lighter than glass and it does not shatter when dropped.
Windows	Polycarbonate	Glass	This polymer makes windows that will not shatter. However, it gets scratched more easily than glass.
Paints	Acrylic	Oil	Acrylic paints do not smell as strongly as oil paints and they do not crack when dry.
Clothes and fabrics	Nylon	Cotton and wool	Nylon is not damaged by heat and water and it can be woven into huge sheets.

polymerized by an addition reaction. These reactions occur when a double bond breaks and forms new single bonds.

The simplest polymer made in this way is polyethylene, known by chemists as polyethene. The monomer of this polymer is ethene (C_2H_4). Ethene has a double bond joining its two carbon atoms. During polymerization, the double bond breaks, and the carbon atoms form a long chain. Each carbon atom is bonded to two other carbon atoms and two hydrogen atoms.

Polyethylene can be made into long, straight chains or branched networks. The straight chains produce a hard and stiff material. Objects made from branched chains are more flexible.

NATURAL AND ARTIFICIAL FIBERS

Our clothes are made from fibers that are woven together. For thousands of years, people used fibers made from natural polymers. For example, wool comes from the fleece of sheep and goats, while cotton fibers are made from the fluff around the seeds of cotton plants.

These natural fibers are often quite short and they have to be spun together to make threads and yarns long enough for weaving into clothing. In the late 19th century, chemists developed ways of making stronger fibers that were made from much longer polymer chains.

The first artificial fiber was made from cellulose, the polymer in wood. Fabric made from cellulose is called rayon. In the 1930s, U.S. chemist Wallace Carothers (1896–1937) invented nylon. Nylon was a completely new polymer made from amines (nitrogen compounds). Nylon has become the most common artificial fiber. It can be made into a huge variety of objects, from silky sheets to the bristles of a brush.

Naming polymers

Other polymers made by addition reactions include polypropene and polystyrene. They are named for their monomers with poly- added at the beginning. Other polymers have very long names almost too long to say! Instead these polymers are known by their initials. For example, PVC stands for polyvinyl chloride. Vinyl chloride is another name for chloroethene (C_2H_3Cl).

Mixing polymers

Polymerization carries on until there are no monomers left. If a new monomer is then added, the chain grows again. This behavior makes it possible to produce copolymers made from two or more different types of monomers.

The properties of a copolymer depend on the different monomers that make it up. Ethene makes soft polymers, while polypropene is tougher. Styrene makes glassy polymers, while rubber polymers are elastic. Chemists can blend these monomers to produce a polymer with just the correct amount of each property. Copolymers can be made from blocks of each monomer, or they can be arranged randomly. Polymers can also be produced with a precise arrangement of monomers. For example, two types of monomers could be arranged one after the other. However, polymers like that are more expensive to produce.

Acrylic fiber is an example of a copolymer. It is a blend of two esters of certain acrylic acids—very reactive types of carboxylic acids.

Wet suits are made of neoprene. This is a waterproof rubber made by addition reactions.

COMMON POLYMERS

You may have heard the names of some common polymers, such as PVC or polyethylene. These compounds and other polymers have a range of different properties. Many of their properties depend on the nature of their monomers. Monomers are the small units that join together to make a long chain. Many plastics are made from a mixture of polymers. Each polymer adds certain characteristics to the plastic.

Polymer	Monomer	Monomer structure	Properties of polymer
Polyethene (polyethylene)	Ethene	Carbon / Hydrogen	Polyethene makes flexible plastics. It is used in packaging and to insulate electrical wires.
Polypropene (polypropylene)	Propene		This polymer makes plastics that are similar to polyethene, but slightly tougher and more expensive.
Polystyrene	Styrene	Phenyl	This polymer is used to make styrofoam. It is also added to other polymers to make them waterproof.
PVC (polyvinyl chloride)	Chloroethene (vinyl chloride)	Chlorine	PVC makes very tough plastics. They are not damaged by fire or strong chemicals and are good insulators.
Teflon (polytetrafluoroethene)	Tetrafluoroethene	Fluorine	Teflon is a very slippery substance that is used in nonstick pans.

Condensation polymers

Some monomers do not form polymers by addition reactions. Instead, they polymerize with a condensation reaction. This reaction produces a molecule of water (H_2O) as the monomers bond together, which is known as condensing.

Nylon, polyester, and the natural polymers cellulose and starch are condensation polymers. Their monomers have two or more functional groups. The monomers join together when the functional groups on each monomer react and form bonds.

The monomers have at least one more functional group, which is not involved in holding the polymer together. These free groups can form bonds with monomers on different polymers. That creates crosslinks between several polymer chains and makes a very strong network.

Polymer properties

When you look at a plastic cup, a rubber ball, or a nylon rope you cannot see the polymers inside them. The polymers are obviously far too small to see. If you could see them, they would not all look the same. For example, a plastic cup is very different from a rubber ball. That is because their polymer chains are arranged in different ways.

The properties of an object made from a polymer depend on how the polymers are arranged. The simplest arrangement is to have polymers that are unbranched and form straight chains. The chains may be many thousands or even millions of atoms in length. A sample of these polymers will contain chains with a wide range of lengths.

Unbranched, straight polymers are packed close together. Some even form crystals. Polymers like that make stiff materials. They do not change shape easily because the polymers inside are packed too closely to move around much.

However, when a sample of this material is stretched, the polymers slip past one another. As a result, the sample becomes longer. When the stretching stops, the polymers stay in their new position, and the sample keeps its new stretched shape. Materials that behave like this are said to be plastic.

A branched polymer has side chains along its main chain. The chains stop polymers from packing together closely. As a result, the polymers are more flexible. Addition polymers, such as polyethylene, can be formed as either straight or branched chains.

Coils and crosslinks

Rubbers are polymers that have coiled chains. When they are stretched, the coils straighten and become longer. However, once the stretching ends, the coiled chains spring back to their original shape. Polymers that behave like that are described as being elastic.

However, untreated rubber behaves like a plastic as well. Some of the polymers slip past each other, causing

A VERSATILE MATERIAL?

You would be right to think that plastic is a very useful type of material. After all it can be made into just about anything. But what happens when we put plastic in the garbage? One of the properties of plastic is that it does not decay easily, so plastics buried along with other garbage remain unchanged for many thousands of years.

Other materials, such as metal or wood, can be recycled or reused. Plastic is more difficult to recycle. Thermosets cannot be melted down at all, and a mixture of different thermoplastics must be separated into their individual types before they can be remolded.

the rubber to stretch permanently. Adding crosslinks between the coils stops that from happening and makes the rubber completely elastic. The process that adds crosslinks to rubber is called vulcanization. This involves adding a curative substance to the rubber, such as sulfur.

Thermosets

Polymers with lots of crosslinks make very rigid materials. For the material to break or change shape, the bonds in the crosslinks must be broken. Many polymers form crosslinks when they are heated. These compounds are called thermosets.

Thermosets are used to make molded objects. The powdered ingredients of the polymer are packed into a mold and heated. The heat makes the thermoset polymers form. The heat also causes crosslinks to connect the polymers making the object very rigid.

Styrofoam is polystyrene pumped full of air bubbles.

CARBOHYDRATES

Biochemistry is the study of the molecules and chemical reactions in living organisms. All life on Earth depends on the chemistry of one element, carbon, and the compounds that it forms.

Candy contains a lot of sucrose, a carbohydrate with a sweet taste. Sucrose is the common white sugar that you can buy as crystals for sweetening drinks such as coffee and tea.

Elements are the basic forms of matter. All elements are made of tiny particles called atoms. When atoms of different elements group together, they form structures called molecules. Living matter uses relatively few of the 92 naturally occurring elements. In fact, most living things are made of only six: carbon, hydrogen, oxygen, nitrogen, sulfur, and phosphorus. Of the rest, only 21 are necessary for biological processes. These occur in tiny amounts, called trace elements.

Carbon is a unique element because it has the capacity to form an almost infinite number of compounds (combinations of different types of atoms). It can do this because carbon has four electrons in its outer shell. These electrons can be shared with other atoms. A whole branch of chemistry, organic chemistry, is devoted to carbon and the compounds it forms.

Among the simplest carbon compounds used by living things are carbohydrates. Carbohydrates are the main source of energy for plants and animals. Carbohydrate molecules consist of one or more bonded saccharides (sugars). The general formula for a carbohydrate is $C_m(H_2O)_n$, where m and n are positive whole numbers greater than or equal to 3 (and can be the same number or different numbers). Carbohydrates have a backbone of carbon to which hydrogen and oxygen atoms are bonded. Because carbohydrates have a backbone of carbon atoms, they are called organic molecules. Although the general formula holds true, some complex carbohydrates have other elements such as sulfur, phosphorus, and nitrogen in their molecules.

Human cells are not able to make carbohydrates from carbon dioxide and water, so we must consume them in our diet. Plants are rich in carbohydrates because plants are able to make these molecules by a process called photosynthesis. For this reason, some types of plants are excellent food sources.

Chemists divide carbohydrates into three classes. The classes are based on the size of the carbohydrate molecule. Monosaccharides have a single (mono) saccharide, disaccharides have two (di), and polysaccharides have many (poly).

Monosaccharides

Monosaccharides, the simplest carbohydrates, include glucose, fructose, galactose, and others such as ribose and deoxyribose, which are components of nucleic acids. The names of many sugars end in -ose by convention. Glucose goes by several names, including dextrose and grape sugar, and it is an extremely important molecule in biology. Glucose is the primary carbohydrate used as energy in humans.

Glucose, fructose, and galactose have the same formula, $C_6(H_2O)_6$, but they are different molecules. The difference is in the arrangement of their atoms. Compounds with the same chemical formula but different arrangements of their atoms are called structural isomers.

Fructose is a very sweet sugar found in honey and fruits. Galactose is in milk. Both fructose and galactose also exist in these foods as constituents of larger molecules called disaccharides.

All female mammals, including primates, produce milk with which they feed their young. Milk contains lactose, a disaccharide sugar made of glucose and galactose.

DRAWING MOLECULES

Chemists have a number of ways of drawing molecules. Below, five carbon (C) atoms and a single oxygen (O) atom are connected in a ring by single bonds shown as straight lines.

Carbon is such a common element in many molecules that sometimes the letter "C" is not shown. This diagram shows the same molecule as left. Other elements, however, such as the single oxygen atom, are still shown. The carbon atoms may also be numbered so that chemists can describe how one molecule connects to another.

In many molecules made of rings or chains of carbon atoms, extra atoms attach to one or more of the carbons.

This diagram shows the same molecule as that immediately left. For simplicity the arrangement of the bonds among the additional carbon, hydrogen, and oxygen atoms is not shown. This is a common method for displaying carbohydrates.

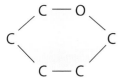

Disaccharides

The bond joining the two saccharides of a disaccharide is called a glycosidic bond. The bond forms when an oxygen and a hydrogen (an –OH, or hydroxyl group) from each saccharide join, making a link through one of the oxygen atoms. This process releases a water molecule and so is termed a condensation reaction.

Important disaccharides include sucrose (glucose + fructose), the component of table sugar and cane sugar, and lactose (glucose + galactose), the main sugar of milk. Although milk is not sweet, it does contain sugar. Not many sugars found in nature are actually sweet. Another disaccharide is maltose, or malt sugar (glucose + glucose). Maltose is sweet tasting, is found in high concentrations in germinating seeds, and is important in beer and whiskey manufacturing.

Polysaccharides

Most carbohydrates are polysaccharides, which are long chains of monosaccharides linked by glycosidic bonds. The three most common polysaccharides are starch, glycogen, and cellulose.

The plants that form the bulk of a cow's diet contain a lot of cellulose. Unlike cows, some plant-eating animals are not able to digest cellulose.

MILK DIGESTION

The human body cannot make use of lactose until it is broken into its saccharide components, glucose and galactose. The breaking of the glycosidic bond is catalyzed (speeded up) by a protein enzyme called lactase. Some adults lack this enzyme and are unable to break down lactose. This condition is called lactose intolerance. People who have this condition cannot consume much milk because the lactose remains in their digestive tract and can cause discomfort and diarrhea.

Carbohydrates are often ingredients of substances that cells can digest, but that is not true of the polysaccharide cellulose, at least not for human cells. Cellulose is one of the most abundant organic molecules on Earth, serving as a structural component of cell walls in plants. Cellulose forms strong, rigid fibers and these fibers give plant cells their strength and help protect them.

Cellulose consists of long, relatively unbranched (straight) chains of glucose. Typically there are a few thousand molecules of glucose in a cellulose polysaccharide. In cellulose, glucose has what is termed a beta configuration. In starch, glucose has an alpha configuration. The difference lies in the positioning of the oxygen atom that bonds the consecutive glucose rings.

To digest cellulose, a biological molecule called an enzyme is needed to break the bonds holding the

TRY THIS

Home Starch Test

Test foods for the presence of starch using this simple method.
Carefully grate a small portion of a vegetable, such as a potato. (Be careful of your fingers!) Put
1 tablespoon of the grated sample in $\frac{1}{4}$ cup of cold water from the faucet and stir.
Then, strain the liquid into an empty cup. Add a few drops of iodine to the liquid. If the iodine turns blue–black, starch is present. Starch will be present in the potato. Can you find it in any other vegetables?

Starch grains stained blue-black with iodine.

which might upset the delicate water balance in the plant.

Plants store starch as an energy source for future use, but in many cases the starch ends up in human stomachs when we consume the plants. Humans can digest starch because we have the enzymes, called amylases, that break down the glycosidic bonds. Amylases work by hydrolysis, which means "breaking down with water." A hydrolysis reaction adds the water molecule lost in the condensation reaction that formed the bond. Adding a water molecule breaks the bond.

Glycogen

Plants store glucose as starch to use as needed. Animals also store glucose, but instead of making starch they make a polysaccharide from glucose called glycogen. Glycogen is stored in liver and muscle cells. Glucose is a source of energy, and the human body must maintain an adequate level of glucose in the blood to nourish cells. When the glucose level falls, which happens between meals, the liver converts glycogen into glucose.

glucose molecules together. The particular type of enzyme needed is called cellulase. Humans cannot digest cellulose because we do not have cellulase in our digestive system. But termites, cows, and a few other animals have cellulase-containing microorganisms in their digestive tract. With the help of these microorganisms, such animals can make a meal of cellulose because their digestive systems can break it down into glucose. Even though people cannot digest cellulose, the fibers are an important part of our diet because they help transport waste material through our digestive systems.

Starch

The primary way plants store carbohydrates for future use is as polysaccharides called starch. These polysaccharides are long chains of glucose molecules, similar to cellulose. However, the glycosidic bonds that hold together the glucose molecules in starch have a different arrangement from the bonds in cellulose.

As far as plants are concerned, an important property of starch is that it is not soluble (it cannot dissolve) in water. Although starch takes up space in a plant cell, it does not cause the cell to draw in water,

SCIENCE WORDS

- **Condensation reaction:** A reaction that produces water, such as when a glycosidic bond is made.
- **Disaccharide:** Carbohydrate made of two saccharide molecules.
- **Glycosidic bond:** A bond that connects one saccharide to another saccharide.
- **Monosaccharide:** Carbohydrate made of one saccharide molecule.
- **Polysaccharide:** Carbohydrate made of many saccharide molecules.
- **Saccharide:** Sugar molecule.

LIPIDS

Lipids are greasy or waxy substances that include fats and oils. Lipids have a variety of structures and perform several different functions in living organisms. They are most important as a source of energy in the body.

It is a well-known fact that oil and water do not mix. There is a chemical reason why that is true: water is a polar molecule (has poles). Water molecules contain two hydrogen atoms and one oxygen atom joined by covalent bonds, in which the atoms share electrons. However, the oxygen and hydrogen atoms do not share electrons equally. The electrons are more attracted to the oxygen atom and pull away from the hydrogen atoms. That has the effect of making the hydrogen ends of the molecule positively charged and the oxygen end negatively charged, like the north and south poles of a magnet. Water is an excellent solvent and will dissolve many substances because its polar molecules attract other charged molecules and pull them apart.

Nonpolar solvents

Nonpolar solvents are made of molecules whose atoms share electrons equally. Since the electrons are spread out uniformly there are no poles (areas of excess charge, either positive or negative). Typical nonpolar solvents include benzene and diethyl ether.

A general rule is that nonpolar substances dissolve in nonpolar solvents. Many lipids are nonpolar, and all lipids contain some nonpolar areas in their structure. However, some lipids contain polar regions that are important to their function and behavior.

Fatty acids

Fatty acids are lipids that have a chain of 12 to 24 carbon atoms with a single carboxyl group attached. A carboxyl group is made of carbon, oxygen, and hydrogen atoms and has the formula $-COOH$. In a saturated fatty acid, all the carbons are joined by single bonds. An unsaturated fatty acid contains one or more carbon-to-carbon double bonds. The double bond means there are fewer hydrogen atoms bonded

SCIENCE WORDS

- **Hydrophilic:** Something that has an attraction to water.
- **Hydrophobic:** Something that does not have an attraction to water.
- **Nutrient:** A substance that provides nourishment to a cell and helps it grow or repair itself.
- **Protein:** A large biological molecule that acts as a structural component of many of the cells of living organisms.

Bees secrete a wax from which they build a honeycomb. Waxes are hard lipids that do not dissolve in water.

to the carbon chain. Saturated fatty acids, which have no carbon-to-carbon double bonds, are therefore saturated (full) with hydrogen atoms. Some of the most common fatty acids have 16 carbons in their chain (for example, palmitic acid) or 18 carbons (such as oleic acid). All natural fatty acids have evenly numbered carbon chains.

The carbon chain of saturated fatty acids is straight, so these fatty acids can stack neatly together. With their closer packing, saturated fatty acids tend to be solid at room temperature. Animal fats tend to be saturated, and therefore solid.

Double bonds between carbon molecules in unsaturated fatty acids cause bends or kinks in the chain. The bends prevent unsaturated fatty acids from packing too closely, so these fatty acids tend to be oils at room temperature. Fats from plants and many species of fish are mostly unsaturated, and therefore they are oily.

TRY THIS

Testing for fats in food

There is a simple method to test a food for the presence of fat. With a circular motion, rub a small amount of food onto a strip torn from a brown paper bag. Try cooking oil first. Place a few drops of water on the bag in a location near the test sample. Hold the paper up to strong light. Both water and the test spot should be transparent. This is because the substances fill spaces between the paper fibers and transmit light.

Wait an hour or so until the water spot has dried, then hold the paper up to the light again. The water spot should no longer be transparent because the water will have evaporated. If the test spot is still relatively transparent, then it contains fat, which does not evaporate as easily as water.

Triglycerides

Although humans and other animals store some energy as glycogen, most of the stored energy is kept in fat cells called adipocytes. The main components of fat cells are triglycerides. A triglyceride consists of a three-carbon molecule called glycerol bonded to three fatty acids. The bond, called an ester bond, forms between a hydroxyl group (–OH) of the glycerol and the –OH of the carboxyl group of a fatty acid. The three fatty acids of many triglycerides are the same, but a triglyceride may have more than one kind of fatty acid. Many of the fats and oils people eat in food are triglycerides.

Phospholipids

Triglycerides are nonpolar and do not dissolve in water. If a phosphate group ($-PO_4$), which is electrically charged, replaces one of the fatty acids, the result is a phosphoglyceride. The general name for a lipid containing a phosphate group is a phospholipid. This molecule has a nonpolar, electrically neutral region (the fatty acids) and an electrically charged polar region (the phosphate group). The oxygen atoms of the phosphate group bond with glycerol and sometimes another polar molecule.

In water, the nonpolar fatty acid "tails" of phosphoglycerides orient away from water molecules since fatty acids are hydrophobic (water hating). But

Most foods contain fatty acids. Saturated fats, such as those in the beef, cheese, and bacon of this hamburger, are bad for the body in large quantities because they are turned into substances that block blood vessels.

the polar "head"—the phosphate group—is hydrophilic (water loving). Phospholipids in water tend to form spherical shapes as the nonpolar tails bunch together on the inside, away from the water molecules, and the polar heads form the sphere's surface.

Cell membranes

A membrane is a thin sheet or covering. The cells of living organisms need membranes to hold in their contents, which include various nutrients and molecules as well as functional structures such as the nucleus. Membranes act as barriers, preventing the cell's contents from disappearing into the surrounding extracellular fluid. Molecules attached to the membrane or embedded inside it regulate the flow of substances into and out of the cell.

Cell membranes have two layers of phospholipids: the phospholipid bilayer. The hydrophilic (water-loving) phosphate groups form the inside and outside surfaces of the membrane and the hydrophobic (water-hating) fatty acid chains form the middle of the membrane. Membranes also contain molecules such as proteins embedded within the phospholipid bilayer. The membrane is not a rigid structure because the phospholipids and embedded proteins can move or flow from one point to another.

OSMOSIS

Osmosis occurs when water (yellow molecules) moves from one solution containing a dissolved substance to another. This process takes place across a semipermeable membrane. The dissolved molecules are too big to cross the membrane.

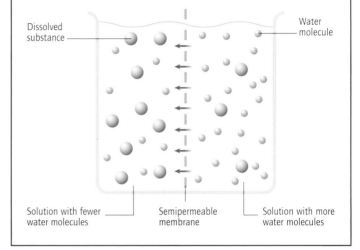

Dissolved substance

Water molecule

Solution with fewer water molecules

Semipermeable membrane

Solution with more water molecules

Membrane diffusion

An important job of a cell membrane is to control and regulate the flow of molecules across it. Membranes block the passage of many substances, but water molecules are small and slip through the phospholipid bilayer by the process of diffusion. Diffusion is the ability of molecules to move about randomly until they are evenly spread out.

Net flows occur when concentrations are different. The fluids inside and outside of the cell contain a wide variety of molecules dissolved in water. The cell membranes allow only certain molecules, such as water, to permeate (cross) the membrane. Such membranes are called semipermeable. If the solution on one side of the cell membrane has a greater number of water molecules than the other, water will diffuse

An animal cell membrane is a double layer of phospholipids called a bilayer. Embedded in the membrane are other molecules, such as proteins, which help substances vital to the cell cross the membrane. They also keep out substances that might harm the cell.

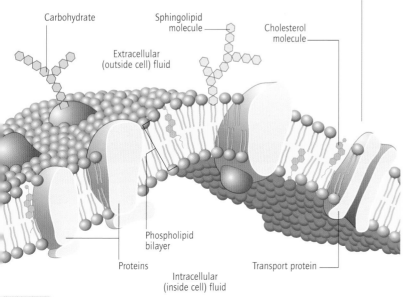

Carbohydrate

Sphingolipid molecule

Cholesterol molecule

Extracellular (outside cell) fluid

Phospholipid bilayer

Proteins

Transport protein

Intracellular (inside cell) fluid

Athletes build muscle naturally through exercise. However, some take artificial steroids that help speed up this process. A number of athletes have been banned from competition after using steroids.

across the membrane to the side where there are fewer water molecules. Eventually, the two sides reach the same concentration. The diffusion of water across a semipermeable membrane is called osmosis. Cells need to keep their interior concentrations equal to those of the exterior, otherwise there is a net flow of water across the membrane. A loss of water causes the cell to shrink, and a surplus swells it to bursting. Both situations damage the cell.

Membrane transport

Large polar molecules and certain highly charged molecules need help to cross the cell membrane. In some cases, special embedded proteins called transport proteins serve as a channel so these molecules can diffuse across the membrane at certain times. Like most diffusion processes, these molecules move from areas where they are in a high concentration to areas where they are low in concentration. But sometimes the cell must transport molecules from areas of low concentration to high, against the natural flow of diffusion. This is called active transport because it needs energy to occur. This energy is derived from various metabolic processes.

Steroids

Nonpolar molecules readily cross cell membranes because they can move in and through the nonpolar layers. Steroids are lipids that perform their function in many cases because they diffuse easily across membranes and get inside the cell. Steroids are often hormones—molecules that travel in the bloodstream and carry messages from cells in one part of the body to another. These derive from the cholesterol lipid. The structure of steroids is entirely different from that of triglycerides and phospholipids; steroids consist of rings of carbon fused to resemble a mesh fence.

THE DANGERS OF STEROIDS

Anabolic steroids are artificial hormones that help muscle growth. Sometimes athletes inject a large amount of anabolic steroids into their bodies in an attempt to increase muscle size and improve their performance. This is a dangerous practice that can result in mental problems and serious physical injuries. Most athletic contests, such as the Olympics, ban these substances.

Proteins and nucleic acids are the most important molecules in the body. They are used as structural molecules to build skin, hair, and muscle. They are also vital for the way the body functions and reproduces cells.

Biochemical molecules are generally large and complex, but they are usually composed of much simpler units that are bonded together. Proteins, for example, are strings of amino acids. Some proteins called enzymes speed up chemical reactions so they occur quickly enough to support life. Other proteins, such as keratin, form rigid structures like horns or fingernails. Regardless of their function, all proteins are made of a sequence of amino acids.

Amino acids

Amino acids are so named because they are made from two groups of atoms, an amino group and a carboxylic acid. Although there are more than 200 types of amino acids, the proteins in most living organisms are made from only 20 amino acids. These are: alanine, arginine, asparagine, aspartate (or aspartic acid), cysteine,

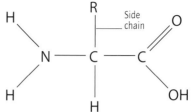

Glycine is the simplest amino acid. Its side chain is made up of a single hydrogen atom. Most proteins contain only small quantities of glycine.

glutamate (or glutamic acid), glutamine, glycine, histidine, isoleucine, leucine, lysine, methionine, phenylalanine, proline, serine, threonine, tryptophan, tyrosine, and valine. Different proteins can have different numbers of amino acids. Small proteins, called peptides, can have fewer than 20 amino acids. One of the largest proteins, titin, which is used in muscle contraction, is a chain of about 27,000 amino acids.

Peptides

Peptides are formed from two amino acids bonded together. A covalent bond joins the carboxyl group of one amino acid and the amino group of another. Proteins are made of a sequence of peptides. A peptide bond forms by a condensation reaction, which is a reaction that releases water (H_2O). The water molecule comes from an OH of the carboxyl group of one amino acid and an H of the amino group of the other amino acid. The side chains are not involved in the reaction. Amino acids contain mostly carbon (C), hydrogen (H), oxygen (O), and nitrogen (N). These elements are the most important in biochemistry, making up about 95 percent of the human body.

Sequence

The structure of a protein is critical to its function. Some proteins are flat and some fold up into balls. Yet all proteins have a three-dimensional structure that is necessary for them to do their job. The structure derives from the protein's sequence of amino acids.

The structure of a protein has four levels—primary, secondary, tertiary, and quaternary. The sequence of amino acids is the primary structure, and this governs the shape of the protein. Interactions among the

---

WHAT IS AN AMINO ACID?

An amino acid consists of a central ("alpha") carbon atom with four attachments. These are:

1) a hydrogen atom

2) a carboxyl group, –COOH (in water this acidic group often loses its positively charged hydrogen atom and becomes COO–, a carboxylate ion)

3) an amino group, –NH_2 (in water this group often gains a hydrogen nucleus and becomes NH_3^+)

4) a side chain, usually designated as R, R_1, R_2, and so on. Amino acids differ from each other because they have different side chains. For example, the side chain for glycine is just –H, and methionine is –CH_4–CH_4–S–CH_4.

The venom of snakes is a mixture of hundreds of proteins, which, in the case of this rattlesnake causes destruction of tissues and the clotting of blood.

amino acids form weak hydrogen bonds. These bonds determine and maintain the protein's shape, or secondary structure. The position (sequence) of the amino acids dictates where these bonds occur. The bonds twist the protein to form a helical segment called an alpha helix or a flattened segment, or beta-pleated sheet.

A protein's tertiary structure reflects the way the alpha helices and beta sheets fold into the protein's shape. In some proteins, this shape is modified by separate chains of amino acids, each with their own tertiary structure. These amino acids change the molecule again to give the final quaternary structure.

Although proteins are large molecules, they are much too small to be seen, even with powerful microscopes. To determine a protein's shape, scientists often use x-ray crystallography.

Function

Many proteins are soluble in water. Most of these proteins are globular (globelike) in shape and perform various functions. An example is hemoglobin, a protein in the blood of mammals. Hemoglobin's job is to carry oxygen to nourish the cells of the body. Hemoglobin has four subunits (separate chains) and contains four iron atoms each capable of binding oxygen.

Other proteins are insoluble in water. These proteins usually consist of long sheets or fibers. An example is collagen, a common protein; about one-third of all protein in

the human body is collagen. Collagen strengthens skin and other tissues. Collagen's insoluble nature is essential for its function—our skin would be of little use if it dissolved in rain!

Nucleic acids

Carbon is vital in biochemistry because it forms long chains of molecules. Proteins are one important group of biochemical molecules. Another important group of molecules are nucleic acids.

A peptide is formed when the carboxyl group of one amino acid bonds with the amino group of another. Water is released during the reaction. Proteins are made up of sequences of peptides.

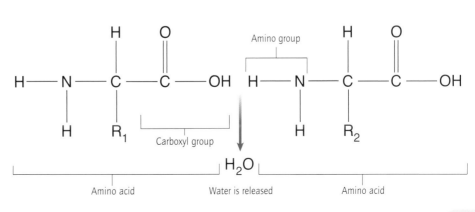

Nucleic acids are strings of chemically bonded molecules called nucleotides. Nucleotides are made of three basic components: a phosphate group, which consists of one phosphorus (P) atom and four oxygen (O) atoms (PO_4^{3-}); a five-carbon sugar such as ribose ($C_5H_{10}O_5$); and a base containing nitrogen. This base can belong to one of two types, purines or pyrimidines. A purine has a five-atom ring structure connected to a six-atom ring, and a pyrimidine has a six-atom ring. Nucleic acids store and transfer information that every cell must have to function. There are two major types of nucleic acids: ribonucleic acid (RNA) and deoxyribonucleic acid (DNA).

RNA

The sugar of RNA nucleotides is ribose and the bases are one of the following: adenine (A) and guanine (G), both of which are purines, and cytosine (C) and uracil (U), both

Adenine   Guanine

Purines

Nitrogenous bases called purines (above) are components of nucleotides. Adenine and guanine are two kinds of purines. Pyrimidines (below) are also components of nucleotides.

Pyrimidines

Thymine   Uracil   Cytosine

TRY THIS

Fruity DNA

Peel and cut a kiwifruit into small pieces and place in a measuring cup. Stir together 0.1 ounce (3 g) of salt, 0.33 fluid ounces (10 ml) of dish-washing liquid, and 3 fluid ounces (100 ml) of water and add to the measuring cup, letting the mixture sit for 15 minutes. Then put the measuring cup in a pan of hot water for 15 minutes. Pour the resulting green liquid in the measuring cup through a kitchen strainer and into a glass.

Carefully pour ice-cold methylated spirits on the back of a spoon over the glass, forming a purple layer on top of the green layer. Leave to stand for at least 30 minutes.

WARNING: Methylated spirits are dangerous and should never be consumed!

Kiwifruit DNA should appear as a white layer between the green and purple liquid. You can fish it out with a loop of wire or a fork.

The DNA of the kiwifruit is visible as a thin white layer between the greenish liquid below and the purple layer above.

of which are pyrimidines. RNA molecules are usually single strands of nucleotides connected by a condensation reaction. The most important aspect of RNA structure is the sequence of bases.

Nucleic acids are named for their association with a cell's nucleus—the structure inside a cell that holds genetic (inherited) information. RNA does not always stay in the nucleus. Three classes of RNA molecules exist: messenger RNA (mRNA) carries information from the nucleus into the cell; outside the nucleus, ribosomal RNA (rRNA) helps make new proteins using mRNA; and transfer RNA (tRNA) helps translate the information carried by mRNA.

DNA

The sugar of DNA nucleotides is deoxyribose, the same as ribose except that one oxygen atom is missing. The bases are the same as RNA with the exception of uracil, which is replaced in DNA by thymine (T). Long strands of nucleotides form DNA molecules.

The normal structure of DNA is a double helix. Single strands of DNA molecules twist around each other like a spiraling ladder. The double helix forms because bases on each strand form weak bonds. A pyrimidine base on one strand bonds with a purine base on another. The double helix is a stable molecule, allowing DNA to exist for long periods without breaking down.

Genes

Segments of DNA and the sequence of bases they carry form genes. Some DNA sequences are genes, and other sequences regulate access to this information. Each double-stranded DNA helix coils around itself and forms a single chromosome in the cell's nucleus. Organisms have various numbers of chromosomes—humans have 23 pairs, mice 20 pairs, and chimpanzees 24 pairs. One of each chromosome pair comes from the mother and one from the father.

Every species (type) of animal and plant has a unique set of genes that defines the structure and function of their cells, tissues, and organs. Many genes come in slightly different sequences called alleles. Genetic differences account for much of the variation in appearance and behavior of species and of individuals within species.

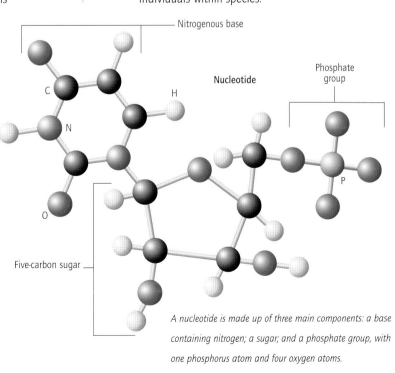

A nucleotide is made up of three main components: a base containing nitrogen; a sugar; and a phosphate group, with one phosphorus atom and four oxygen atoms.

METABOLIC PATHWAYS

Metabolism refers to changes brought about by the many chemical reactions occurring in the cells of living organisms. Many of the reactions follow a series of steps called a metabolic pathway.

One of the most important changes produced by metabolism is the conversion of food to energy. People need energy to run and jump and even to do very gentle activities such as reading and thinking. Cells, of course, need energy to support these activities as well as many others. This energy comes from food, which must be broken down by the body before it can be used.

Energy

Energy is always conserved (cannot be lost), but it can be transformed into other forms of energy. Potential energy is stored energy, while kinetic and thermal (heat) energy are energies of motion. Chemical reactions that produce thermal or kinetic energy from potential energy are exothermic reactions. Some reactions, called endothermic, do the opposite. To say that a reaction "consumes energy" usually refers to transforming potential energy into motion.

TRY THIS

Enzymes and apples

Ripe apples contain enzymes, including one called polyphenoloxidase. This enzyme catalyzes the reaction of oxygen with some of the compounds in the apple. The resultant reaction produces dark products and makes the apple turn brown.

Like all reactions, including those catalyzed by enzymes, temperature affects the rate at which the reaction occurs. Cut an apple in half; place one half in a refrigerator and leave the other uncovered at room temperature. Examine the apple halves every 20 minutes for two hours. Note the rates of the reaction under the two different conditions by observing the color of the apple.

Exothermic reactions occur readily, and once they begin most do not need any help to carry on. This is similar to the process of diffusion, which takes place as molecules spontaneously move from high to low concentrations. An example of an exothermic reaction is the burning of gasoline in the presence of oxygen.

Endothermic reactions generally require an "input" of thermal or kinetic energy to proceed. These

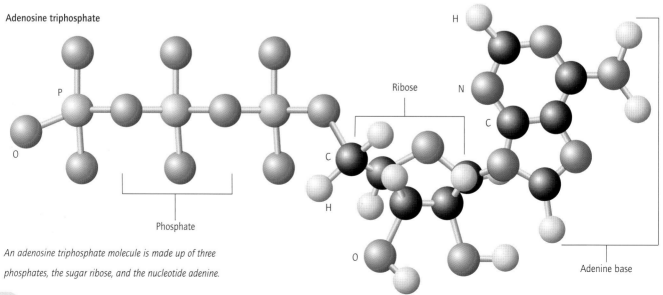

Adenosine triphosphate

An adenosine triphosphate molecule is made up of three phosphates, the sugar ribose, and the nucleotide adenine.

reactions transform thermal energy into potential energy. Thus, energy is stored in the chemicals, and their bonds, that are made by the reaction. An example of an endothermic reaction is the conversion of two molecules of ammonia (NH_3) into nitrogen, N_2, and hydrogen, $3H_2$.

Some reactions in cells are exothermic, and some are endothermic. The way cells manage their energy "budget" is to use a go-between—a molecule that can be generated by exothermic reactions and then consumed by endothermic reactions. The molecule that acts as the go-between is called adenosine triphosphate (ATP).

Adenosine triphosphate

ATP consists of the nucleotide adenine, ribose, and a chain of three phosphates. Cells must maintain adequate levels of this molecule to survive. The cell makes ATP by adding a phosphate group to adenosine diphosphate (ADP). This reaction is called phosphorylation.

ATP is often considered the cell's energy currency. ATP is a medium of energy exchange, like money to be exchanged for goods and services. The bonds holding the phosphate groups on the end of the molecule contain potential energy. When endothermic reactions are needed, ATP molecules become involved. The ATP molecules are broken down, and the potential energy stored in their bonds is released.

With the aid of ATP, biochemical reactions can occur as their products become needed. However, providing energy alone is not sufficient to support life. The chemical reactions of cells must take place at the required speed. Thus, cells require enzymes to catalyze (speed up) reactions, controlling the rate at which the reactions generate their products.

The enzyme lactase is often used in the manufacture of ice cream to give a sweeter taste and a smoother texture. Ice cream without lactase feels "sandy."

Enzymes

Most enzymes are globular (globelike), water-soluble proteins that either float around or are attached to some part of the cell. An enzyme participates in a reaction, making it go faster, but the reaction does not change the enzyme. The enzyme takes part in the reaction many times and chemically remains the same throughout.

In almost all cases, an enzyme catalyzes only one specific reaction. This feature of enzymes is called specificity. The enzyme binds a substrate—one of the reactants that is changed in the reaction—and holds it in the proper place and position. Enzymes are often named after the reaction

they catalyze or the reactants they bind. The name ends in the suffix –ase. For example, the enzyme lactase catalyzes the breakdown of the sugar lactose, which occurs in milk.

Carbohydrate catabolism

Enzymes speed up all kinds of reactions in the body. Some of the most important involve carbohydrate catabolism—the breaking down (catabolism) of carbohydrates. This process provides energy by making ATP molecules. Fats and proteins also provide energy, but carbohydrates are the easiest kinds of food for the body to digest. After a meal, the digestive system breaks the bonds of polysaccharides, converting them into molecules of glucose or fructose, which are transported around the body in the blood. Then the process of making ATP begins.

Glycolysis

The first pathway in carbohydrate catabolism in the body's cells is glycolysis. This series of nine different reactions splits a six-carbon glucose molecule into two three-carbon molecules called pyruvate. The process generates two molecules of ATP and two molecules of nicotinamide adenine dinucleotide (NADH). NADH is another biomolecule that effectively stores potential energy in its bonds. The NADH molecules play an important role later, in another pathway.

Glycolysis is an anaerobic process, which means that it does not require oxygen. However, glycolysis extracts only about 2 percent of the energy in glucose molecules. This means that there is a great deal of potential energy left in glycolysis products.

The energy left over from glycolysis is usually not wasted. Many organisms, including people, extract additional energy from the glycolysis products by aerobic (oxygen-using) pathways. However, certain simple organisms such as bacteria and yeast extract additional energy by an anaerobic process called fermentation. For instance, certain microorganisms extract energy from grains or fruit and produce carbon

GLYCOLYSIS

Glycolysis is a series of biochemical reactions in which glucose is broken down to pyruvate. Energy is stored as molecules of adenosine triphosphate (ATP). Energy has to be introduced to the glucose to get the reactions started, and again at step 3; this is called activation energy and is provided by molecules of ATP. Then, a sequence of reactions occurs. The final products of glycolysis are the acid pyruvate and ATP. If glycolysis starts with one molecule of glucose and two molecules of ATP, the products are two molecules of pyruvate and eight molecules of ATP.

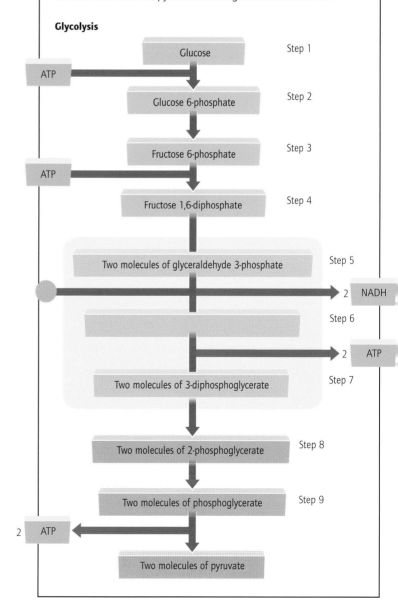

Glycolysis

Glucose	Step 1
ATP	
Glucose 6-phosphate	Step 2
Fructose 6-phosphate	Step 3
ATP	
Fructose 1,6-diphosphate	Step 4
Two molecules of glyceraldehyde 3-phosphate	Step 5
	2 NADH
	Step 6
	2 ATP
Two molecules of 3-diphosphoglycerate	Step 7
Two molecules of 2-phosphoglycerate	Step 8
Two molecules of phosphoglycerate	Step 9
2 ATP	
Two molecules of pyruvate	

dioxide and ethanol (alcohol). This is a process that brewers and winemakers have taken advantage of for thousands of years. Fermentation may also occur in our muscle cells when we exercise.

Storing energy

The food we eat supplies glucose, the starting point of glycolysis. Our cells are constantly in need of energy, especially at times of high activity, but we do not have to eat constantly. The body maintains glucose levels by several methods. One way of raising the glucose level is by breaking down glycogen, which is a storage molecule that contains many glucose molecules bonded together. Another way to obtain glucose is through gluconeogenesis.

Mitochondria

Most cells in the bodies of people and animals contain an aerobic pathway for squeezing more energy from

Brewers rely on fermentation to make beer. Yeast is added to a mixture of malt, hops, and water, and fermentation produces energy, carbon dioxide, and beer.

TRY THIS

Making Gas

You can buy some yeast at the grocery store and carry out your own fermentation experiments.

Crush two or three cookies and place the pieces in a sealable bag. Add 1 tablespoon of yeast and about ¼ cup of warm water to the bag. Mix the contents by shaking.

Squeeze all of the air out of the bag and seal it, then put it in a warm place. After half an hour the bag should have swollen.

The gas produced is carbon dioxide—one of the products of fermentation. You can also try this experiment with sugar, flour, baked beans, and cereal.

Which one produces the most gas?

the products of glycolysis. These reactions occur in structures contained within cells called mitochondria. Mitochondria have an inner and outer membrane and are shaped like tubes or cylinders.

Citric acid cycle

The pathway for aerobic metabolism is called the citric acid cycle. This series of reactions takes the slightly modified products of glycolysis and extracts even more energy, using oxygen and releasing carbon dioxide. These reactions are the reason we breathe in oxygen and exhale carbon dioxide.

The transition between glycolysis and the citric acid cycle occurs when pyruvate, the product of glycolysis, undergoes a reaction. The reaction turns pyruvate into an acetyl group ($-COCH_3$) that binds to a molecule

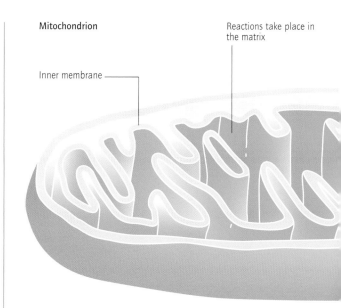

Mitochondrion — Reactions take place in the matrix

Inner membrane

Energy production within a cell is called cellular respiration. It takes place within the cell's mitochondria. Mitochondria are enclosed by two membranes and are usually sausage-shaped. When a molecule of pyruvate enters a mitochondrion, a sequence of reactions takes place in the matrix. These reactions produce ATP.

FAT AND HEALTH PROBLEMS

Adipocytes are cells that have much of their volume taken up by fat. Fat adds a lot of weight to the body and can make exercise harder. Too much stored fat also contributes to health problems such as high blood pressure and heart disease. The only sure way to lose weight is to decrease food intake and to exercise more. A lower level of food intake forces the body to use up stored energy sources, and the body increases its use of triglycerides during times of heavy activities such as exercise.

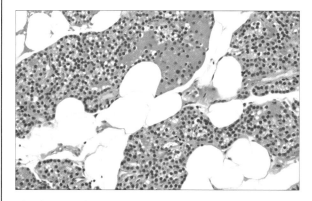

The white areas of this adipocyte cell are deposits of fatty triglycerides. The purple region is the cell's nucleus.

---

called coenzyme A (CoA). The result is acetyl CoA, the starting point of the citric acid cycle.

The citric acid cycle is cyclical because its starting point—acetyl CoA—is also the end point. The pathway is a loop consisting of eight reactions (steps), each catalyzed by an enzyme.

Only one of the reactions of the citric acid cycle makes ATP, and it produces only a single molecule of ATP. Other products of the cycle are three molecules of nicotinamide adenine dinucleotide (NADH) and a molecule called flavin adenine dinucleotide ($FADH_2$).

Electron transport

NADH and $FADH_2$ are reducing agents, which means they donate electrons in chemical reactions. They give these electrons, originally from glucose molecules, to acceptors (oxidizing agents). In the process, NADH and $FADH_2$ are oxidized, becoming NAD^+ and FAD, respectively. (NAD^+ and FAD take part in the citric acid cycle, where they are reduced again to NADH and

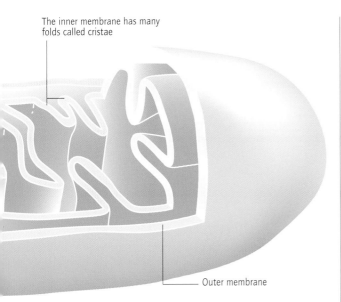

The inner membrane has many folds called cristae

Outer membrane

SCIENCE WORDS

- **Carbohydrate:** One of a group of compounds that includes sugars, starch, and cellulose.
- **Enzyme:** A protein that speeds up chemical reactions in organisms.
- **Fatty acid:** A compound made up of an unbranched hydrocarbon chain with an even number of C atoms and a carboxyl group.
- **Hydrolysis:** The process by which a molecule splits after reacting with a molecule of water.
- **Triglyceride:** A major component of fats. They are a concentrated food energy store in organisms.

FADH$_2$, respectively.) Molecules embedded in the inner membrane of mitochondria pass the electrons along a chain, called the electron transport system.

The electron transport system takes energy from the electrons as they move along the chain. The energy gained by this process pumps hydrogen ions across the inner membrane. As the hydrogen ions diffuse back, their movement drives an enzyme called ATP synthase. This adds a phosphate group to the ADP to generate ATP. The electron transport system normally yields another 32 molecules of ATP per glucose molecule. The total production of ATP from glycolysis, the citric acid cycle, and the electron transport system is on average

36-38 molecules of ATP per initial glucose molecule. That is about 40 percent of the available energy.

Fatty acid metabolism

Fats are a rich source of energy, providing more than twice as much energy as the same weight of carbohydrate. Some of the energy derived from food is not immediately needed, and the body stores this energy as triglycerides in adipocytes. Triglycerides are "burned" as needed, particularly during exercise.

Triglycerides produce much energy; for example, a molecule of a fatty acid called palmitic acid yields 129 molecules of ATP.

Amino acid metabolism

The citric acid cycle is important not just in breaking down (catabolizing) molecules and extracting energy, but also in anabolic (building up) reactions. The citric acid cycle is involved in building up as well as breaking down amino acids.

The primary function of amino acids is to make proteins. Excess amino acids from the diet are not stored by the body, and a portion of these molecules can be broken down into products that take part in the

Hans Krebs

Hans Krebs (1900-1981) was born in Germany but moved to England in 1933 after the Nazi government ended his job. In the late 1930s Krebs used his expert knowledge of enzymes and chemical reactions to discover the details of the citric acid, or Krebs, cycle. In 1953 he won a share of the Nobel Prize in Physiology or Medicine for his outstanding contributions to biochemistry. He was knighted (giving him the title "Sir") in 1958.

citric acid cycle. The amino acids are oxidized and used as an energy source. After a prolonged time without food, the body will begin to break down its own proteins and convert the amino acids into energy in a desperate effort to sustain life. The opposite reactions can also occur. Then, enzymes catalyze reactions in which molecules involved in the citric acid cycle and other pathways are made into amino acids.

Nucleotide metabolism

Nucleotides are components of many important substances of the body, such as the nucleic acids RNA and DNA. Unlike many of the molecules of life, however, we do not get many of these vital nucleotides from our diet. Instead, several amino acid pathways are involved in making nucleotides.

Right: Trees and other green plants use sunlight to make carbohydrates from carbon dioxide and water. This process is called photosynthesis, and it also makes the oxygen that animals need to live.

Photosynthesis takes place in chloroplasts, which are tiny organs within plant cells. They make the leaves look green. Within chloroplasts, chlorophyll absorbs sunlight, and light reactions produce ATP and NADPH. Elsewhere in the chloroplast, a series of dark reactions fix carbon dioxide from the air and produce carbohydrates. The equation for photosynthesis is:

$6CO_2 + 6H_2O + light \rightarrow C_6H_{12}O_6 + 6O_2$

Photosynthesis uses light energy to convert carbon dioxide and water into carbohydrate (glucose) and oxygen. Compare this reaction to respiration, the process by which animals derive energy from the oxidation of carbohydrate:

$C_6H_{12}O_6 + 6O_2 \rightarrow 6CO_2 + 6H_2O$

Plants harness the energy of sunlight and transform it into chemical potential energy and oxygen. Animals obtain energy from the reverse process, breaking apart the bonds of carbohydrate, producing energy, carbon dioxide, and water.

Photosynthesis

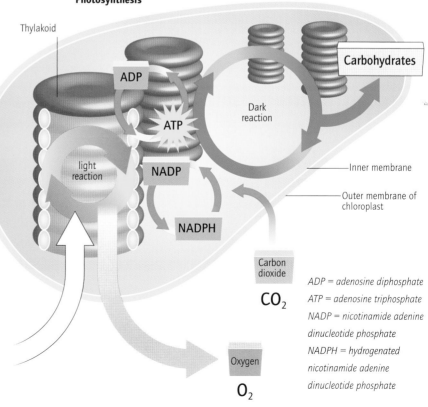

Thylakoid

ADP

ATP

light reaction

NADP

NADPH

Dark reaction

Carbohydrates

Inner membrane

Outer membrane of chloroplast

Carbon dioxide

CO_2

Water

H_2O

Oxygen

O_2

ADP = adenosine diphosphate
ATP = adenosine triphosphate
NADP = nicotinamide adenine dinucleotide phosphate
NADPH = hydrogenated nicotinamide adenine dinucleotide phosphate

Photosynthesis

The reactions that break down glucose and generate ATP liberate a great deal of potential energy (stored energy). Energy cannot be created or destroyed, only changed from one form to another. So it must take a great deal of energy to make glucose molecules. The energy to do this comes from sunlight.

Photosynthesis is a metabolic pathway in green plants, algae, and a few bacteria and other single-celled organisms. The word *photo* means "light," and *synthesis* means that the light energy is used to make, or synthesize, substances. Photosynthesis makes carbohydrates and ultimately the food that fuels all living organisms on the planet.

Right: Plants need nitrogen to make proteins. Most plants get nitrogen from the soil in which they grow. However, since Venus flytraps live in bogs, where the soil has little nitrogen, they do things differently. They get their nitrogen directly from insects that they catch and digest in their leaves.

SCIENCE WORDS

- **Amino acid:** A compound made up of a carboxyl group (–COOH) and an amino group (–NH_2) attached to the same C.
- **ATP:** A nucleotide that carries chemical energy in living organisms. It is made up of an adenine base, ribose, and three phosphate groups.
- **Nucleotide:** A molecule made up of a nitrogen-containing base, a sugar, and a phosphate group.

Photosynthesis begins with light-absorbing molecules called chlorophyll. Other light-absorbing substances are also involved. Chlorophyll and its associated molecules occur inside plant cells inside tiny organs called chloroplasts. Many of a plant's cells have these structures, but they are especially active in leaves.

Plants use sunlight to make ATP and electron-carrier molecules called nicotinamide adenine dinucleotide phosphate (NADPH). Then comes a series of reactions called dark reactions (because they do not involve light). These reactions involve a cycle called the Calvin cycle (named for its discoverer, American chemist Melvin Calvin, 1911–1997). The reactions store the chemical energy in a more stable, long-lasting form of carbohydrate molecules for future use.

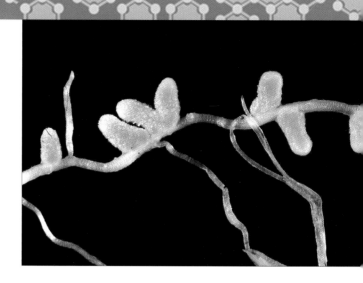

Chemical reactions occurring in or around cells synthesize (make) most of the critical molecules of life, including molecules required for storing and interpreting genetic (inherited) information.

Before the 19th century, many people believed that chemical reactions in the body and other living things were somehow different from the reactions that take place in the laboratory of chemists. Some people thought there was a special force involved in the making of biochemical molecules that was only present in living tissue. If so, there would be no way to synthesize biochemical molecules outside of the body's tissues. Then in 1828, a German chemist, Friedrich Wöhler (1800–1882), synthesized urea, a product of protein metabolism, which is excreted in the urine. Shortly afterward chemists began synthesizing many other organic compounds in their laboratories, proving that no vital force was required for any of these compounds.

Synthesis of amino acids

Amino acids are the building blocks of proteins. Twenty different amino acids are used to make proteins in most living organisms. For humans, 11 of these amino

Friedrich Wöhler

Friedrich Wöhler (1800–1882) was a German chemist and professor at the University of Göttingen in Sweden from 1836 until his death. He was a devoted teacher, often starting his classes very early in the morning, and wrote several chemistry textbooks. By making the compound urea from an inorganic salt, ammonium cyanate, Wöhler helped show that the principles governing biochemical molecules are the same as those for other substances. He also isolated the elements aluminum and silicon.

acids can be synthesized in the body. (Sometimes more or fewer amino acids can be synthesized, because of differences in children and adults and the existence of alternative pathways.)

Nitrogen is an important component of amino acids that people obtain from food. Almost all of this nitrogen originally came from plants. Plants obtain nitrogen from the air—about 80 percent of air is nitrogen. Bacteria living in the soil or attached to the roots of certain plants "fix" nitrogen (incorporate the element into usable compounds). The nitrogen fixation process involves the turning of atmospheric nitrogen, which exists as the molecule N_2, into ammonia (NH_3). This process occurs with the help of a large enzyme called nitrogenase. The ammonia quickly becomes ionized and plants use this reactive substance in the synthesis of amino acids and other nitrogen-containing molecules. Like photosynthesis and carbohydrate production, nitrogen fixation is another reason why plants are vital to all life on Earth.

The 11 amino acids that the body can synthesize are called nonessential amino acids, since they are not essential in the diet. These amino acids are often made using molecules involved in other metabolic pathways, particularly the citric acid cycle. Glutamate and glutamine, two of the amino acids that can be synthesized by humans, are the starting point for making many of the nonessential amino acids as well as other important molecules. These two amino acids

The pink nodules on these pea plant roots are filled with bacteria. The bacteria fix nitrogen from the atmosphere and convert it into an organic form that the plant can use to produce proteins.

are so critical that all living organisms have the enzymes glutamate dehydrogenase and glutamine synthetase, which catalyze the synthesis of glutamate and glutamine, respectively.

Making lipid membranes

A cell needs a membrane to keep the cell's interior separated from the solution that surrounds it, as well as to regulate the traffic of molecules into and out of the cell. Cell membranes are largely made of lipids called phospholipids. The body must ensure that it has sufficient quantities of phospholipids in order to grow and maintain its tissues. Although membranes are broken down and recycled, synthesis is also important.

The chemical phosphatidate is a simple phosphoglyceride, a common type of phospholipid. Phosphatidate is involved in several pathways that synthesize more complex phosphoglycerides, which are components of cell membranes. Phosphatidate is also often involved in the synthesis of triglycerides, the fats in which the body stores energy. Phosphatidate itself comes from a molecule called glycerol 3-phosphate by

How do new bean plants know how to grow? The answer lies in the bean seed, which contains all the information and instructions for making the chemicals that make up a bean plant.

a series of reactions involving coenzyme A. Coenzymes are small molecules that are needed to help some enzymes work. "A" denotes that this molecule supplies an organic group that the enzyme needs to function. Coenzyme A has a key role in the citric acid cycle.

Synthesis of nucleotides

Nucleotides are the building blocks of deoxyribonucleic acid (DNA) and ribonucleic acid (RNA). Both of these molecules carry genetic information. Like lipids in cell membranes, old nucleotides are often recycled. When cells disassemble old or unneeded RNA or DNA, the nucleotides usually go into making new molecules of RNA or DNA. Synthesizing nucleotides from their basic components costs the cell more energy than recycling old molecules, but sometimes this is necessary.

Genetic information

The long chains of nucleotides that make up the nucleic acids RNA and DNA are part of the cell's method of storing genetic information and carrying out its instructions. The process of storing,

maintaining, and acting on genetic information involves molecular synthesis on a large scale and in a precise manner. The sequence of nucleotide bases in RNA and DNA contains information that must be preserved during synthesis of these long molecules. The cell uses these sequences as templates to synthesize the many different proteins it needs to carry out its function. The flow of genetic information goes from DNA, which holds the information, to RNA, which transmits it to the enzymes that synthesize proteins.

Most of a human cell's DNA resides in the nucleus, the central structure of a cell. Growth of tissues involves cell division, since cells grow and form new tissue by dividing into two, producing two cells. When a cell divides, its DNA must replicate (copy itself) so that both daughter cells have the same DNA as the parent cell.

DNA replication

Replicating DNA involves making new DNA. This synthesis does not proceed at random. Because the DNA's sequence contains information, the sequence must be preserved as much as possible. This need to maintain the

This food pyramid shows the different food groups and the relative amount from each group to eat for a healthy diet. People who eat a balanced diet will get all the amino acids needed by the body. Extra sugar and fat should only be eaten in small amounts.

sequence is important: The sequence must be copied exactly or the wrong proteins will be produced.

Prior to cell division, the cell replicates its DNA and forms it into X-shaped structures called chromosomes. Chromosomes are long, coiled strands of DNA that carry genetic information. Replicating the base sequence involves pulling apart the double-helix structure of DNA. That is not difficult because the strands are bonded with weak hydrogen bonds instead of strong covalent ones. After they are separated, each strand becomes a template for building its double-helix partner. A large enzyme called DNA polymerase binds to each of the strands and attaches the correct nucleotide, slowly moving down the chain. (The enzyme gets its

Fats and Sugars

Dairy

Fish and Meat

Vegetables

Fruit

Carbohydrates

name because it helps polymerize DNA nucleotides, which means it catalyzes the reaction by which nucleotides link together to form a polymer.) When the enzyme is finished there are two identical double-helix DNA molecules (if there were no errors in copying).

Each strand of a DNA double helix can serve as the template because the two strands are complementary—the sequence of one strand determines the other. That occurs because adenine (A) bases always bond to thymine (T) bases, and cytosine (C) bases always bond to guanine (G) bases, and this makes the most stable double-helix structure. If you know the sequence of one strand of a double helix you can always determine the other: the complementary strand of the sequence AAGCAT, for example, is TTCGTA.

DNA repair

Most of the time, DNA polymerase attaches the correct nucleotide base. However, there are sometimes errors in copying, so a base pair in a DNA double helix is mismatched: An A is not bonded to a T, or a C is not bonded with a G. Unintentional changes in the sequence can also occur if the DNA molecule becomes damaged: perhaps a molecule that readily engages in chemical reactions causes a change in one of the nucleotides, or radiation strikes the DNA and breaks the molecule apart. Changes in the DNA sequence are called mutations.

Since the cell relies on information contained in the sequence of DNA, it must try to correct errors. The complementary strands aid error detection because in many situations where there are mismatched pairs, one of the nucleotide bases is correct and the other is an accidental change or a copying error. Figuring out which base is the correct one is not always easy, but sometimes the mistaken base has been chemically altered. Newly copied strands are often chemically tagged, so the cell knows which strand is most likely to contain a copying error. Enzymes in the cell catalyze actions that detect and correct sequence mistakes. Some, but not all, mistakes are found and corrected.

GEL ELECTROPHORESIS

Gel electrophoresis is a technique that scientists use to separate out mixtures of proteins or nucleic acids. Proteins and nucleic acids are large, heavy molecules that have side chains of compounds that form ions in solution. Ions have a positive or negative electrical charge because some atoms in the molecule have gained or lost electrons. When an electric current is passed through a solution, ions move toward the oppositely charged electrode.

Several drops of mixed protein or nucleic acid solution are applied to the middle of a gel plate that has a positive electrode at one end and a negative electrode at the other. When a current is applied, the molecules are either attracted or repelled by the electrodes, depending on their charge. The gel acts like a molecular sieve that separates out the molecules according to how heavy they are. The lightest molecules are able to move through the gel fastest and will get closest to the relevant electrode. After a set period of time, the current is turned off and the plate is rinsed with a staining fluid. The molecules are revealed as a series of bands or spots. Each molecule travels a certain distance according to its mass and charge. The spots on the gel can then be sampled and examined chemically to determine which protein or nucleic acid is which.

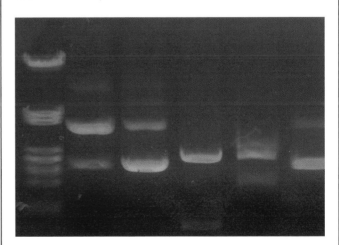

A gel electrophoresis plate showing six types of DNA. The column on the left is a mixture of known markers, used for comparison. The different bands signify different fragment sizes. The brighter the band, the higher its concentration.

Genes and DNA

Extremely important sequences of DNA form genes, a unit of genetic information. Genes control or influence features such as eye color, height, and certain types of behavioral tendencies. A gene does this by coding for a specific protein. Proteins perform many of the functions of the cell and are also involved in structural properties, so the number and type of these proteins strongly influences how cells behave and interact with one another. The behavior of the cells in turn governs the features of the organism.

MICROARRAYS

Humans have about 23,000 genes. One way to study a cell is to examine the specific genes that it expresses (transcribes). With thousands of possibilities this can be a daunting task, but tools called microarrays make it easier. A microarray contains a large number of single-stranded DNA genes or gene segments attached to a small glass slide or membrane. When the contents of a cell are poured over the microarray, specific mRNA molecules bind with the corresponding gene on the microarray. Microarrays give scientists a quick method of determining which genes have been expressed, because the location of each gene on the slide is known.

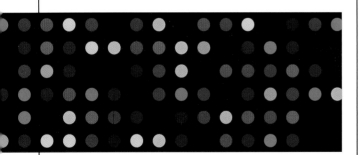

A microarray, sometimes called a biochip, consists of a glass slide holding dots of DNA. Each dot contains a different piece of DNA that will bind to a specific gene in the sample being tested. The microarray is scanned by a laser, which highlights dots that have reacted. The colors indicate which genes are present in the sample.

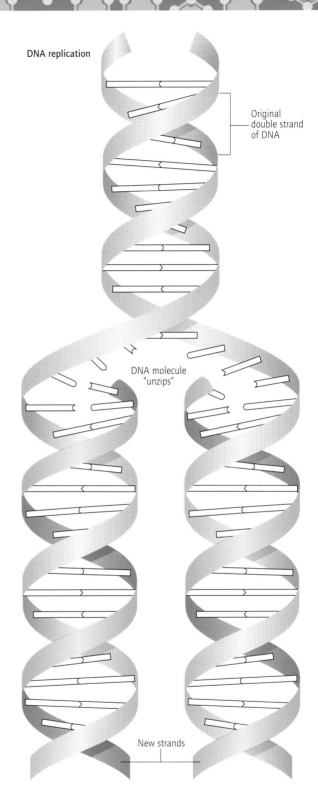

DNA replication

Original double strand of DNA

DNA molecule "unzips"

New strands

When DNA replicates, the original double strand of the molecule breaks apart so each strand can be copied. The new strands are identical to the original double helix.

This wallaby is white and has pink eyes because its genes lack the code for the usual brown wallaby hair and eye colors. The mother has passed on these features to her baby.

Enzymes "read" the sequence of a gene to make the corresponding protein. First, a group of molecules in the cell copies the sequence of DNA, which resides in the nucleus. Special RNA molecules called messenger RNA (mRNA) carry this information out of the nucleus to the molecules that are responsible for synthesizing proteins. The process of producing these mRNA molecules is called transcription.

Transcription

An enzyme called RNA polymerase catalyzes the synthesis of mRNA. DNA provides the template. RNA polymerase first binds to a DNA sequence referred to as a promoter. The promoter positions the enzyme in the correct spot on the correct strand, and guides it in the proper direction to read the code. The process is similar to DNA replication, since RNA polymerase generates a complementary strand and preserves the information in the sequence of the gene. However, the synthesized strand is RNA, and because RNA does not use thymine bases, a uracil (U) base replaces thymine in the sequence.

Each gene is located on a specific area of a chromosome. The chromosomes in a cell fall into pairs and each member of a pair carries genes for the same feature. Thus, cells have two forms of each gene, although the two genes may be slightly different versions, or alleles. One allele came from the mother and one from the father. Sometimes cells transcribe only one of these two, and sometimes both, depending on which gene is involved.

Almost all cells in the body contain a full set of chromosome pairs. The exceptions include red blood cells, which do not have any (none are needed in these cells because they have short lifetimes), and reproductive cells such as sperm and eggs, which have only one chromosome of each pair. The union of a sperm and egg during reproduction provides the full set, one of each pair coming from the father's sperm cell and one from the mother's egg cell.

Although cells of the body have the same genes, there are major differences in the cells composing various organs. Cells have special functions. Muscle cells contract, for example, while brain cells transmit

SCIENCE WORDS

- **Base pair:** A base and its partner in a strand of nucleic acid. These are always adenine and thymine (or uracil), and guanine and cytosine.
- **Double helix:** The shape of a DNA molecule. It resembles a twisted ladder.
- **Polymerase:** An enzyme that creates a polymer (long chain) of nucleotides from a template of DNA or RNA.

messages to one another. These functions depend on the production of proteins that perform the required tasks. Cells from muscle, brain, liver, skin, and other organs are different not because they have different genes, but because they transcribe, or express, a differently ordered set of proteins. The proteins from the set of transcribed genes carry out the cell's special function.

Translation

The process of synthesizing a protein coded by the mRNA sequence is called translation. Translation occurs in ribosomes, complex cellular structures containing three subunits of ribosomal RNA (rRNA) and dozens of different proteins. Ribosomes translate the mRNA by "reading" each three-base portion of the sequence as a code for the making of a specific amino acid. The amino acids are attached to molecules of transfer RNA (tRNA). Each type of tRNA carries one of the 20 different amino acids. Translation is a complex operation. Enzymes catalyze each step as the ribosome moves along the mRNA, synthesizing the protein according to the coded instruction.

Each three-base segment of the mRNA is called a codon, and it codes for a specific amino acid. This code is called the genetic code, because it is how genes

transmit their information. RNA consists of four different bases, so each of the three positions in a codon can have one of four different bases or "letters"—A, C, U, or G. Changing the sequence of bases gives the possibility of 64 different codons or "words" in the genetic code.

Ribosomes accept the mRNA as a correct copy of the gene. If this is not true, the ribosome produces a protein with an incorrect sequence. Such proteins generally do not have the proper shape to perform their function, so mutations in the gene sequence produce an incorrect or abnormal protein. On rare occasions the new protein may fulfill a new and beneficial role, but much more often the protein is useless or even harmful.

Each codon represents either an amino acid or a start or stop instruction. When the ribosome encounters the GGG code, it inserts the amino acid glycine into the protein sequence. Enzymes associated with the ribosome catalyze the peptide bond that attaches the glycine to the previous amino acid of the growing chain. The codon AUG codes for the amino acid methionine as well as signaling the beginning of the protein. The codons UAA, UGA, and UAG signal the ribosome to stop translating.

SCIENCE WORDS

- **Allele:** An alternative version of a specified gene.
- **Chromosome:** A long, coiled molecule of DNA that carries genetic information.
- **Codon:** A sequence of three nucleotide bases that codes for an amino acid.
- **Peptide bond:** The bond that forms when two amino acids join.
- **Reproduction:** The biological process by which a new generation of plants or animals is created.

These plums have been genetically modified to be resistant to plum pox. This virus can otherwise be eliminated only by destroying the infected tree, which has significant economic impact on the grower.

Molecules of tRNA identify the amino acid they carry by having a three-base sequence in their nucleotides that is complementary to the amino acid's codon. This sequence is called an anticodon. For example, the codon AAC codes for asparagine, and a tRNA molecule with the anticodon UUG carries an asparagine amino acid. The anticodon binds to the mRNA codon coding for the proper amino acid, positioning the tRNA so the ribosome can snatch its amino acid and add it to the chain. The tRNA then falls off and picks up another molecule of its amino acid, ready to participate in another reaction.

DNA recombination

Cells do all they can to maintain their DNA sequences. However, in some situations there is a benefit to shuffling the genes of the chromosomes, which is called DNA recombination.

During reproduction, the offspring receives one chromosome of each pair from each parent. When these chromosomes are rejoined in the offspring, the DNA is recombined so that it takes some sections from one parent and some sections from the other parent.

SHUFFLING THE GENE PACK

Shuffling genes is nature's way of ensuring the survival of species. Both parents have two sets of chromosomes, but provide only one set of chromosomes to the offspring. Which set the offspring receives is entirely random. The genes on the chromosomes are mixed up again when the DNA is copied. Some are taken from one parent and some from the other. In this way, new adaptations occur that may give the organism an advantage over competitors.

POLYMERASE CHAIN REACTION

Forensic scientists working at a crime scene used to find it difficult to obtain enough biological material on which to carry out DNA tests. However, even the most microscopic samples can now be tested using a technique called the polymerase chain reaction (PCR). This method makes multiple copies of a single DNA sequence.

When a cell divides, it uses enzymes called polymerases to copy the DNA in its chromosomes. PCR uses the same method. The first step is to heat the DNA sample so the two strands of DNA unzip. As they separate, a polymerase taken from a high-temperature bacterium makes a copy using each strand as a template. However, the polymerase cannot begin to copy the strand unless a short sequence of nucleotides is already present to start the process. Another enzyme is used as a primer to build this first sequence, but the sample has to be cooled for this to happen. The temperature is then raised again to allow the polymerase to copy the sequence.

This cycle, which takes about two minutes, is repeated up to 30 times. Because each copied sequence can act as a new template, at the end of the process there are 1 billion new pieces of DNA. These pieces can then be used as markers to look for similar fragments in other samples. If they match, then scientists know they have a likely suspect.

This is nature's way of "experimenting," with the goal of producing the best possible combination of genetic features for the survival of the offspring.

DNA recombination requires the breaking of DNA strands. A large segment or just a small portion of one chromosome crosses over to the other of the pair, and then the strands join up with their new partner. The chromosome pair swaps parts, both large and small.

Mixing of genes in recombination occurs naturally, but scientists have learned how to manage a similar procedure. Recombinant DNA technology alters or manipulates the genes of an organism, sometimes producing a new kind of plant or animal.

GLOSSARY

Acid A compound that splits easily into a positively charged hydrogen ion and another negatively charged ion.

Aldehyde A compound with a carbonyl group attached to the end of its molecule.

Alkane A hydrocarbon chain in which all atoms are connected by single bonds.

Allele An alternative version of a specified gene in a chromosome.

Allotrope One form of a pure element.

Amino acid A component of a protein made up of a carboxyl group (–COOH) and an amino group (–NH$_2$), both attached to the same carbon (C) atom.

Atom The smallest piece of an element that still retains the properties of that element.

ATP A nucleotide that carries chemical energy in living organisms. It is made up of an adenine base, ribose, and three phosphate groups.

Base pair A base and its partner in a strand of nucleic acid. These are always adenine and thymine (or uracil), and guanine and cytosine.

Benzene A ring of carbon atoms in which some electrons are shared by all atoms in the molecule.

Biochemistry The study of chemical reactions inside bodies.

Bond An attraction between atoms.

Carbohydrate One of a group of compounds that includes sugars, starch, and cellulose.

Carbonyl A functional group made by a carbon atom connected to an oxygen atom by a double bond.

Chemical equation Symbols and numbers that show how reactants change into products during a reaction.

Chromosome A long, coiled molecule of DNA that carries genetic information.

Codon A sequence of three nucleotide bases that codes for an amino acid.

Combustion The reaction that causes burning and is generally a reaction with oxygen in air.

Compound A substance formed when atoms of two or more different elements bond together.

Condensation reaction A reaction that produces water, such as when a glycosidic bond is made.

Covalent bond A bond in which two or more atoms share electrons.

Crosslink A bond between two polymers.

Crystal A solid made of regular repeating patterns of atoms.

Deoxyribonucleic acid (DNA) The molecule that contains the genetic code for the functioning and reproduction of all cellular organisms

Disaccharide Carbohydrate made of two saccharide molecules.

Double helix The shape of a DNA molecule. It resembles a twisted ladder.

Elastic Describes substances that return to their original shape after being stretched.

Electron A tiny particle that makes up part of an atom. Electrons have a negative charge.

Electron shell A layer of electrons that surrounds the nucleus of an atom.

Enzyme A protein that speeds up chemical reactions in organisms.

Ester A compound formed when an alcohol reacts with a carboxylic acid.

Ether Compound in which two hydrocarbon groups are joined by an oxygen atom.

Evaporate To turn from liquid to gas.

Fatty acid A compound made up of an unbranched hydrocarbon chain with an even number of carbon (C) atoms and a carboxyl group (–COOH).

Fermentation A reaction in which sugar is turned into ethanol.

Functional group The section of an organic molecule that gives it certain chemical properties.

Glycosidic bond A bond that connects one saccharide to another saccharide.

Hydrocarbon A type of organic compound that contains only atoms of carbon (C) and hydrogen (H.

Hydrolysis The process by which a molecule splits after reacting with a molecule of water.

Hydrophilic Something that has an attraction to water.

Hydrophobic Something that does not have an attraction to water.

Hydroxyl A functional group made up of an oxygen and a hydrogen atom.

Inorganic Describes any substance that is not organic.

Ion An atom or molecule that has lost or gained one or more electrons and has become electrically charged.

Keratin A type of protein that forms structures such as fingernails and horns.

Ketone A compound with a carbonyl group attached in the middle of its molecule.

Molecule Two or more atoms connected by chemical bonds.

Monosaccharide Carbohydrate made of one saccharide molecule.

Nucleic acid A chain of nucleotides.

Nucleotide A molecule that is made up of a nitrogen-containing base, a sugar, and a phosphate group.

Nucleus The central core of an atom containing protons and neutrons.

Nutrient Any substance that provides nourishment to a cell and helps it survive, grow or repair itself.

Organic Describes a compound that is made of carbon and generally also contains hydrogen.

Peptide bond The bond that forms when two amino acids join.

Periodic table A table that organizes all the chemical elements into a simple chart according to the physical and chemical properties of their atoms. The elements are arranged by atomic number from 1 to 116.

Polymerase An enzyme that creates a polymer (long chain) of nucleotides from a template of DNA or RNA.

Polymerization The process that makes monomers join together to make polymers.

Polysaccharide Carbohydrate made of many saccharide molecules.

Protein A large biological molecule made of amino acids. Proteins act as structural components of many cells.

Reproduction The biological process by which a new generation of plants or animals is created.

Ribonucleic acid (RNA) Molecule that carries genetic information. It controls how a cell functions and reproduces.

Saccharide A sugar molecule.

Triglyceride A major component of fats, tryglycerides provide a concentrated food energy store in organisms.

Vitamin An essential substance an organism needs for good health.

FURTHER RESEARCH

Books

Atkins, P. W. *The Periodic Kingdom: A Journey into the Land of Chemical Elements.* New York, NY: Barnes & Noble Books, 2007.

Bendick, J., and Wiker, B. *The Mystery of the Periodic Table (Living History Library).* Bathgate, ND: Bethlehem Books, 2003.

Berg, J. *Biochemistry.* New York, NY: W. H. Freeman, 2006.

Brown, T. E. *et al. Chemistry: The Central Science.* Englewood Cliffs, NJ: Prentice Hall, 2008.

Cobb, C., and Fetterolf, M. L. *The Joy of Chemistry: The Amazing Science of Familiar Things.* Amherst, NY: Prometheus Books, 2010.

Davis, M. *et al. Modern Chemistry.* New York, NY: Holt, 2008.

Gray, Theodore. *Theo Gray's Mad Science: Experiments You Can Do at Home—But Probably Shouldn't.* New York, NY: Black Dog & Leventhal Publishers, 2009.

Greenberg A. *From Alchemy to Chemistry in Picture and Story.* Hoboken, NJ: Wiley, 2007.

Herr, N., and Cunningham, J. *Hands-on Chemistry Activities with Real-life Applications.* Hoboken, NJ: Jossey-Bass, 2002.

Karukstis, K. K., and Van Hecke, G. R. *Chemistry Connections: The Chemical Basis of Everyday Phenomena.* Burlington, MA: Academic Press, 2003.

Lehninger, A., Cox, M., and Nelson, D. *Lehninger's Principles of Biochemistry.* New York, NY: W. H. Freeman, 2008.

LeMay, E. *et al. Chemistry: Connections to Our Changing World.* New York, NY: Prentice Hall (Pearson Education), 2002.

Levere, T. H. *Transforming Matter: A History of Chemistry from Alchemy to the Buckyball.* Baltimore, MD: The Johns Hopkins University Press, 2001.

Oxlade, C. *Elements and Compounds (Chemicals in Action).* Chicago, IL: Heinemann, 2008.

Poynter, M. *Marie Curie: Discoverer of Radium (Great Minds of Science).* Berkeley Heights, NJ: Enslow Publishers, 2007.

Saunders, N. *Fluorine and the Halogens.* Chicago, IL: Heinemann Library, 2005.

Shevick, E., and Wheeler, R. *Great Scientists in Action: Early Life, Discoveries, and Experiments.* Carthage, IL: Teaching & Learning Company, 2004.

Stwertka, A. *A Guide to the Elements.* New York, NY: Oxford University Press, 2002.

Thompson, B. T. *Illustrated Guide to Home Chemistry Experiments: All Lab, No Lecture.* Sebastopol, CA: O'Reilly Media, 2008.

Tiner, J. H. *Exploring the World of Chemistry: From Ancient Metals to High-speed Computers.* Green Forest, AZ: Master Books, 2000.

Trombley, L., and Williams, F. *Mastering the Periodic Table: 50 Activities on the Elements.* Portland, ME: Walch, 2002.

Walker, P., and Wood, E. *Crime Scene Investigations: Real-life Science Labs for Grades 6–12.* Hoboken, NJ: Jossey-Bass, 2002.

Wilbraham, A., *et al. Chemistry.* New York, NY: Prentice Hall (Pearson Education), 2001.

Woodford, C., and Clowes, M. *Routes of Science: Atoms and Molecules.* San Diego, CA: Blackbirch Press, 2004.

Web sites

The Art and Science of Bubbles
www.sdahq.org/sdakids/bubbles
Information and activities about bubbles.

Chemical Achievers
www.chemheritage.org/classroom/chemach/index.html
Biographical details about leading chemists and their discoveries.

The Chemistry of Fireworks
library.thinkquest.org/15384/chem/chem.htm
Information on the chemical reactions that occur when a firework explodes.

Chemistry: The Periodic Table Online
www.webelements.com
Detailed information about elements.

Chemistry Tutor
library.thinkquest.org/2923
A series of Web pages that help with chemistry assignments.

Chem4Kids
www.chem4Kids.com
Includes sections on matter, atoms, elements, and biochemistry.

Chemtutor Elements
www.chemtutor.com/elem.htm
Information on a selection of the elements.

Eric Weisstein's World of Chemistry
scienceworld.wolfram.com/chemistry
Chemistry information divided into eight broad topics, from chemical reactions to quantum chemistry.

General Chemistry Help
chemed.chem.purdue.edu/genchem
General information on chemistry plus movie clips of key concepts.

IUPAC
www.iupac.org/
Web site of the International Union of Pure and Applied Chemistry.

Molecular Models
chemlabs.uoregon.edu/GeneralResources/models/models.html
A site that explains the use of molecular models.

New Scientist
www.newscientist.com/home.ns
Online science magazine providing general news on scientific developments.

The Physical Properties of Minerals
mineral.galleries.com/minerals/physical.htm
Methods for identifying minerals.

Scientific American
www.sciam.com
Latest news on developments in science and technology.

Virtual Laboratory: Ideal Gas Laws
zebu.uoregon.edu/nsf/piston.html
University of Oregon site showing simulation of ideal gas laws.